The Black Box

WITH KWAME ANTHONY APPIAH

Encyclopedia of Africa

The Dictionary of Global Culture

Africana: The Encyclopedia of the African and African American Experience

Encarta Africana

WITH KEVIN M. BURKE

And Still I Rise: Black America Since MLK

WITH JENNIFER BURTON

Call and Response: Key Debates in African American Studies

WITH EVELYN BROOKS HIGGINBOTHAM

African American National Biography

WITH FRANKLIN W. KNIGHT

Dictionary of Caribbean and Afro–Latin American Biography

WITH NELLIE Y. McKAY

The Norton Anthology of African American Literature

WITH HOLLIS ROBBINS

In Search of Hannah Crafts: Essays on the Bondwoman's Narrative

The Norton Annotated Uncle Tom's Cabin

The Portable Nineteenth-Century African American Women Writers

WITH CORNEL WEST

The African-American Century

The Future of the Race

WITH DONALD YACOVONE

The African Americans: Many Rivers to Cross

The Black Box

WRITING THE RACE

Henry Louis Gates, Jr.

PENGUIN PRESS

NEW YORK

2024

PENGUIN PRESS
An imprint of Penguin Random House LLC
penguinrandomhouse.com

LIBRARY OF CONGRESS CATALOGING-IN-PUBLICATION DATA
Names: Gates, Henry Louis, Jr., author.
Title: The Black box : writing the race / Henry Louis Gates, Jr.
Other titles: Writing the race
Description: New York : Penguin Press, 2024. |
Includes bibliographical references and index.
Identifiers: LCCN 2023034918 (print) | LCCN 2023034919 (ebook) |
ISBN 9780593299784 (hardcover) | ISBN 9780593299791 (ebook)
Subjects: LCSH: African Americans—Race identity—History. | African
Americans—Intellectual life—History. | United States—Race
relations—History. | African Americans in literature.
Classification: LCC E185.625 .G38 2024 (print) | LCC E185.625 (ebook) |
DDC 908.996/073—dc23/eng/20230823
LC record available at https://lccn.loc.gov/2023034918
LC ebook record available at https://lccn.loc.gov/2023034919

Printed in the United States of America
1   3   5   7   9   10   8   6   4   2

Designed by Amanda Dewey

For Stephanie Gates
Always outside of the box

For Eleanor Margaret Gates-Hatley
Always remember you have the right
to check your own box, or no box at all

... be ye not entangled again with the
yoke of bondage.

GALATIANS 5:1

Race is the modality in which class is
lived, the medium through which
class relations are experienced.

STUART HALL, *Policing the Crisis*, 1978

Contents

CONTENTS

The Black Box

All my life I had been looking for something, and everywhere I turned someone tried to tell me what it was. I accepted their answers too, though they were often in contradiction and even self-contradictory. I was naïve. I was looking for myself and asking everyone except myself questions which I, and only I, could answer.

It took me a long time and much painful boomeranging of my expectations to achieve a realization everyone else appears to have been born with: That I am nobody but myself.

RALPH ELLISON, *Invisible Man*

My granddaughter, Ellie, was born by C-section on a Saturday afternoon in November of 2014, after her mother, my older daughter, Maggie, stoically suffered through induced labor for about twenty-four hours. That evening, my son-in-law, Aaron Hatley, came over for a warm hug and a celebratory shot of bourbon from my oldest bottle of Pappy Van Winkle's Family Reserve. I listened to Aaron's play-by-play of the previous day's events, and after a decent pause, I asked the question that I had wanted to ask all along:

"Did you check the box?" I asked, apropos of nothing we had just discussed.

Without missing a beat, my good son-in-law responded, "Yes, sir. I did."

"Very good," I responded, as I poured a second shot of Pappy Van Winkle.

Aaron, a young white man, had checked the "Black" box on the form that Americans are required to complete at the time of the birth of a child. Now, my daughter's father's admixture—in other words, mine—is 50 percent sub-Saharan African and 50 percent European, according to the tests offered by commercial DNA companies that I have taken over the last decade and a half. My son-in-law is 100 percent European. Because my daughter is 75 percent European, her daughter, Ellie, will test about 87.5 percent European when she spits in the test tube. "Legally," at least once upon a time—and if not "legally" any longer, then by convention, practice, and/or volition—Eleanor Margaret Gates-Hatley, who looks like an adorable little white girl, will live her life as a "Black" person, because her father and mother checked the "Black" box. (I imagine that our conservative Supreme Court, which has already weighed in on the use of such boxes in higher education admissions, will continue to have its eye on them.) And because of that arbitrary practice, a brilliant, beautiful little white-presenting female will be destined, throughout her life, to face the challenge of "proving" that she is "Black," simply because her self-styled "race man" grandfather ardently—and perhaps foolishly—wished for her racial self to be socially constructed that way.

Such is the absurdity of the history of race and racial designations in the United States of America, stemming from "the law of hypodescent," the proverbial "one-drop rule." Perhaps Eleanor will choose to dance the dance of racial indeterminacy, moving effortlessly back and forth across the color line. Or maybe she will claim a social identity that reflects the percentage of her ancestors over the last five hundred years who were of European descent. Or maybe she will keep a photograph of her grandfather in her pocketbook, and delight in refuting—or affirming, as the case may be—the sheer, laughable, tragic arbitrariness of the social construction of race in America. The most important thing is that this be her choice.

By now, most of us are all too familiar with requests to

check this kind of box. We also know all too well what the search for the "black box"—the flight recorder—sadly signifies in the event of a crash. That device preserves a record of the truth amid disastrous circumstances: it is what survives. For me, the black box is also a powerful metaphor for the circumscribed universe of being within which people of African descent were forced to attempt to construct a new identity after emerging on this side of the Atlantic after the horrors of the Middle Passage, transported here on an inhumanely cramped slave ship—another circumscribed enclosure, another black box of sorts—to provide the labor to create an economic order that would fundamentally reshape the economies of Europe and the emerging United States. But it also is a resonant metaphor for the social and cultural world that they created within this circumscribed space—the people the abolitionist Martin R. Delany named "a nation within a nation," and whom the great scholar W. E. B. Du Bois called "a small nation of people."[1]

For me, this figurative black box is a concept that is quite useful for understanding the history of African Americans in this country, similar in resonance to the haunting metaphor "the Veil" coined by Du Bois in his classic 1903 work *The Souls of Black Folk*. The black box has a long and curious history both inside and outside of

Black letters. And like all metaphors, its significations have multiplied through its long life.

It was the Yale legal scholar Stephen L. Carter who defined it in the manner most closely related to that box that my son-in-law checked, which will define so very many of Ellie's choices, from small, seemingly insignificant things to the manner in which her application to college is treated to how her physician will think of her risks for certain medical conditions. Carter defined his own box in this way:

> To be black and an intellectual in America is to live in a box. So, I live in a box, not of my own making, and on the box is a label, not of my own choosing. Most of those who have not met me, and many of those who have, see the box and read the label and imagine they have seen me. The box is formed by the assumptions others make when they learn that I am black, and a label is available for every occasion.[2]

In Carter's usage, the black box is a place of identity confinement through predefinition, akin to the late literary critic Barbara Johnson's brilliant definition of a stereotype as "an already read text."[3] The Black face walks into the room, and at a glimpse, the viewer knows all that they need to know already about the person wearing the mask of Blackness. Blackness is a veritable repository of African American historical meta-identity, a box containing a long list of connotations, significations, stereotypes, folklore, myths, jokes, boasts, assumptions, predispositions, and counterclaims.

Good luck, Carter is suggesting, shedding any of those connotations, which one can only do by unwriting what has already been inscribed, and thus is always already being read just as soon as that Black face is glimpsed.

Standard uses of the idea of the black box trace back to the early 1930s, according to the *Oxford English Dictionary*, connoting "a device which performs intricate functions but is not readily understood." By the end of World War II, at the latest, "a black box system" is one with an input and an output but whose internal workings are not comprehensible.

The black box, in other words, is something whose internal workings we can't know about, but whose output we can see, touch, hear, feel, or see. While we can determine inputs, and while we can measure outputs, we can have no way to determine how these outputs are produced.

I find this metaphor a useful analytical tool for thinking about both the nature of the discursive world that people of African descent have created in this country— behind Du Bois's Veil, as it were—and how this very world has been "seen" and "not seen" from outside of it, by people unable to fathom its workings inside. The black box, in this sense, is reminiscent of Milton's uncanny description of hell's fearsome furnace, which, even in that fiery black hole's endless darkness, mysteriously manages to irradiate:

> . . . a great Furnace flam'd, yet from those flames
> No light, but rather darkness visible.
> (*Paradise Lost*, 1:62–63)

One way to think about the history of African Americans is by reflecting upon the marvelously baffling and ingenious means by which they have navigated their way in and out of an impenetrable black box that they have created, one in which they have both willingly and unwillingly (like my granddaughter), perplexingly and bewilderingly, been confined. My focus here in this book on the legacy of self-definition over the long course of Black intellectual history since the eighteenth century is my attempt to tell the story of the black box, the story, literally and figuratively, of writing the race. The chapters in the body of the book all had their origin in my lectures for the Introduction to African American Studies class I have taught at Harvard for many years. These are the themes that have long fascinated me—haunted me, in some cases— to which I have returned again and again.

Perhaps the first black box of all was the definition of

Africa as "the Dark Continent," a metaphor for the color of its inhabitants' skin as well as for their supposed benightedness, a continent devoid of beauty, truth, and especially reason. This metaphor was used to justify the second, even crueler black box within which people of African descent found themselves placed by Europeans, the dreadful transatlantic slave trade, responsible for perhaps the largest forced migration in human history. The fugitive slave author Henry Box Brown literalized this trope by escaping from slavery in 1849 by being shipped from Richmond to Philadelphia in a box measuring three feet one inch long, two feet six inches high, and two feet wide. The box was labeled "this side up" to keep Brown upright, but the instruction was often ignored, meaning Brown spent hours of his trip upside down in this small box. He drank water from a beef bladder and received air through three holes he had drilled in the box.[4]

This black box of literal confinement was thus always mirrored by a place of figurative storage, the repository of the racist stereotypes employed initially to justify the enslavement of a continent of human beings and then, subsequent to the abolition of slavery, employed again with renewed vigor and efficacy because of dramatic developments in technology, to justify the rollback of Reconstruction and the rise of Jim Crow segregation precisely when the formerly enslaved were doing their damnedest to climb out of the black box of slavery. Ostensibly banned or forced underground, these stereotypes live on.

But the black box was also, somehow, a place of sublime creativity, a universe of culture mysteriously and inexplicably produced, often unintelligible to those outside of it. Frederick Douglass was one of the first to recognize this when he mused about the magical ways in which enslaved men and women composed the spirituals, the sublime compositions that Du Bois aptly named the "Sorrow Songs":

> While on their way [to the Great House], they would make the dense old woods, for miles around, reverberate with their wild songs, revealing at once the highest joy and the deepest sadness. They would compose and sing as they went along, consulting neither time nor tune. The thought that came up, came out—if not in the word, in the sound;—and as frequently in the one as in the other. They would sometimes sing the most pathetic sentiment in the most rapturous tone, and the most rapturous sentiment in the most pathetic tone.[5]

Most important, Douglass tells us, was the fact that these songs were composed in code, music set "to words which to many would seem unmeaning jargon, but which, nevertheless, were full of meaning to themselves"—to those fluent in the language forged and spoken in the black box.[6] Thomas Wentworth Higginson remarked on "Negro Spirituals" as "strange plants," which, until the Civil War, he "had before seen in museums alone," outside of the box, along with "the rhythmical barbaric dance the negroes call a 'shout,' chanting, often harshly, but always in the most perfect time, some monotonous refrain."[7] How in the world were these cultural artifacts being created? it was asked. What is the source of these symbolic languages forged within this conceptual black box, languages that needed to be interpreted by observers outside of the box to be fully "heard," to be understood?

Not even all of the enslaved could read these signs. As Douglass confesses, "I did not, when a slave, understand the deep meaning of those rude and apparently incoherent songs. I was myself within the circle; so that I neither saw nor heard as those without might see and hear. They told a tale of woe which was then altogether beyond my feeble comprehension; they were tones loud, long, and deep; they breathed the prayer and complaint of souls boiling over with the bitterest anguish. Every tone was a testimony against slavery, and a prayer to God for deliverance from chains."[8] What to the nonliterate were merely "wild notes," to those within the black box able to decipher the code were utterances voiced in another language. The list of sublime cultural artifacts created from within the black box is long and continues to grow. When the bandleader James Reese Europe introduced jazz to Europeans during World War I, French musicians demanded to know through what tricks and devices the bandleader's musicians were creating the sounds coming from their instruments, since European instruments couldn't make those sounds.[9]

For Booker T. Washington, Douglass's self-appointed successor, the black box was not a "box" at all, but a barrel, a metaphor no doubt taken from his years as a student in Hampton Institute in the Tidewater region of Virginia, a barrel filled with crabs, each crab hell-bent on keeping every other crab contained within the confines of that barrel. As Marcus Garvey noted, suggesting that he had felt the pain of the claws of fellow crabs swimming in that barrel:

> Most of the trouble I have had in advancing the cause of the race has come from negroes. Booker Washington aptly described the race in one of his lectures by stating that we were like crabs in a barrel, that none would allow the other to claim over, but on any such attempt all would continue to pull back into the barrel the one crab that would make the effort to climb out. Yet, those with vision cannot desert the race, leaving it to suffer and die.[10]

For W. E. B. Du Bois, the black box was an extended discourse mischievously misnamed "the Negro Problem," a discourse imposed on the Black community by apologists justifying the eradication of rights gained during Reconstruction, set in motion by the Harvard paleontologist and geologist Nathaniel S. Shaler in the pages of *The Atlantic* in 1884 and continuing through the late nineteenth century and well into the twentieth. It was this box that Du Bois and his peers found themselves trying to write their way out of, as it were, as he poignantly puts it in *The Souls of Black Folk*:

> Between me and the other world there is ever an unasked question: unasked by some through feelings of delicacy; by others through the difficulty of rightly framing it. All, nevertheless, flutter round it. They approach me in a half-hesitant sort of way, eye me curiously or compassionately, and then, instead of saying directly, How does it feel to be a problem? they say, I know an excellent colored man in my town; or I fought at Mechanicsville; or, Do not these Southern outrages make your blood boil? . . . To the real question, How does it feel to be a problem? I answer seldom a word.
>
> And yet, being a problem is a strange experience. . . . [11]

Du Bois described the black box as a place of suffocating confinement, a place in which "[t]he shades of the prison-house closed round about us all: walls strait and stubborn to the whitest, but relentlessly narrow, tall, and unscalable to sons of night who must plod darkly on in resignation, or beat unavailing palms against the stone, or steadily, half hopelessly, watch the streak of blue above."[12] It was to free himself and the race from the bounds of this box that he wrote and spoke so prolifically, addressing the subject again and again, seemingly tirelessly, over the full range of genres, outlets, and platforms. But by 1934 at the latest, Du Bois had become keenly aware that a strategy of liberation based on negation could only take him so far. Being doomed to repudiate the pernicious assertions of the Other was a trap. If the master defines all the terms, where does that leave the bondsman? That was the problem, as Wole Soyinka pointed out with devastating efficiency, with the philosophy of *Négritude*. And that was the problem with all of those unwanted Black dolls in Kenneth and Mamie Clark's famous "doll test" that played such a key role in the success of *Brown v. Board of Education*.[13]

Du Bois's Veil was a two-way mirror that lined the walls of the black box, allowing the Negro to see out while remaining invisible to observers outside. Du Bois's fellow Harvard graduate and sometime ideological foe, the philosopher Alain Locke, extends the mirror imagery. Even "the thinking Negro" inside the black box forged "in the mind of America," he wrote, is forced "to see himself in the distorted perspective of a social problem. His shadow, so to speak, has been more real to him than his personality."[14]

And what of the legacy of the first discursive black box, that pernicious discourse of race and reason whose lines were stenciled during the Enlightenment by Hume and Kant and Jefferson? It had only morphed down through the decades in a variety of reprehensible forms, including academic "histories" of the period that were thinly veiled racist propaganda, and assuming its most popular and vulgar forms in extremely popular white supremacist novels such as Thomas Dixon, Jr.'s, *The Leopard's Spots: A Romance of the White Man's Burden, 1865–1900* (1902) and *The Clansman: A Historical Romance of the Ku Klux Klan* (1905), which D. W. Griffith adapted into the wildly popular and unremittingly racist film *The Birth of a Nation* (1915). Du Bois summed up this rhetorical onslaught with devastating succinctness:

> The Negro has long been the clown of history; the football of anthropology; and the slave of industry.[15]

For Richard Wright, the black box is a hideout for the hero of *The Man Who Lived Underground*. For Wright's successor Ralph Ellison, in *Invisible Man*, the black box is both a boxing ring in which two blindfolded Black boys are forced to beat each other senselessly in order to win the fight's prize and also, famously, the hole underground in which Ellison's protagonist hides away from a world that seeks to impose its masks of identity upon him, where he types the manuscript that we eventually are surprised to learn that we are reading over his shoulder. When Dr. Martin Luther King, Jr., had the audacity to insert himself into the morality of American involvement in the Vietnam War, even—or especially—several of his fellow leaders of the civil rights movement publicly told him that he was out of bounds, demanding that he redirect his concerns to issues relevant to those doomed to dwell within the black box, advice that the good reverend boldly ignored.

More recently, the figure of a box as a term or condition of "Blackness" is used quite effectively in Dawn Lundy Martin's *Life in a Box Is a Pretty Life*, which explores enclosure from a Black and queer perspective, and Terrance Hayes's *Wind in a Box*, whose poem "The Blue Seuss" perhaps explores the metaphor of the black box at its fullest:

> Blacks in one box
> Blacks in two box
> Blacks on
> Blacks stacked in boxes stacked on boxes

Blacks in boxes stacked on shores
Blacks in boxes stacked on boats in darkness
Blacks in boxes do not float
Blacks in boxes count their losses

. . .

Blacks in voting booths are
Blacks in boxes
Blacks beside
Blacks in rows of houses are
Blacks in boxes too[16]

This is a book about some of the key debates that Black people have had with one another, within the black box, about its nature and function, but mostly about how to escape from it. I conceived of the content of the Introduction to African American Studies lecture course, out of which most of the chapters of this book grew, as a way of introducing students to the often disregarded fact that Black people have actually been arguing with one another about what it means to be Black since they began to publish their thoughts and feelings in the latter quarter of the eighteenth century. The moral of the class, and of this book, is that there never has been one way to be Black; that African Americans are as varied and as complex in their political and religious beliefs, let's say, and in their cultural and religious practices as any other people are.

And they voiced those internal differences, as it were, with great fervor and passion, stunning eloquence, and vehemence, often engaging those Black thinkers with whom they disagreed with enmity and intensity, and even the nastiest and pettiest ad hominem attacks. Within the long tradition of Black discourse, the political, as we shall see, could be quite personal.

Because a black box is something we can't know about, as it were, these debates within and about the African American tradition for too long have been opaque to most Americans, in the same way that the songs of his enslaved sisters and brothers remained opaque to Frederick Douglass. Too often, we talk about "the Black community" like it's a village composed of a unitary group, one with shared experiences and unified concerns and views. But there are as many ways of being Black as there are Black people. And the tradition of Black thought is most correctly described as a series of contentions, often fiery ones. But then fire, as the greatest Black intellectuals have always known, can generate light as well as heat.

I believe that a necessary intervention is demanded at a time of increasing focus on identity and identity politics in the latest iteration of the so-called culture wars. Reflecting at once on what binds Black Americans together and on what distinguishes individuals and subcultures within that tradition seems to me quite critical at this pivotal, bitterly contested moment, as polarization and the bubble effect of cable news and social media have led so many of us to lazily think of every group as monolithic, be it a voting group, a consuming group, or a behaving group. This book attempts to show that in the case of the world that has unfolded within the black box, *this has never been true*. But the metaphor also applies to Black discourse responding to itself: something is a "black box" when it is unknowable, and within the conceptual box labeled "Blackness," as this book attempts to show, the "right" answer about how to escape the black box has never been formulated or voiced, precisely because there never has been, and never will be, *one right answer* to that haunting question.

Consider this paradox: "Blackness" was an arbitrary category invented by Europeans and Americans in the Enlightenment to justify the horror show of Black subjugation. The human beings who suddenly became "Black" were then forced to play a complex game of "representation" to claim some space in the world, and that vexed process has evolved into an incredibly rich, nuanced, and profound legacy of self-definition within this diverse and amazing community composed of every type of person living on the planet Earth, some fifty million of them in this country alone, connected by being in relationship to this proverbial black box, a metaphysical construct invented to justify an economic order in which their selfhood could be objectified, their subjectivity robbed, and their labor stolen.

The black box signifies a twinned, paradoxical reality: the very concept of "race" is the child of *racism*; it is the figurative black box in which people of African descent were, and continue to be, confined, so as to justify the caste subordination manifesting itself in the Big Bang of the transatlantic slave trade, which oiled the emerging international capitalist network. But at the same time, these devalued human beings had to make a home within this box and claim their humanity within that cruelly delimited, claustrophobic space, in no small part at first by playing the Enlightenment's game of using the master's tools—what we might think of as the "literacy of writing"— to *inscribe themselves* into the discursive arena, and then increasingly finding their own autonomous space within which their own conversations became interior ones, written for and directed to the community itself, but that also interacted with the larger culture where power needed to be claimed, or at least the attempt to claim power most urgently needed to be made.

Against the odds, some of the first Black authors during the Enlightenment managed to forge successful careers and live out their lives comfortably. I'm thinking of

Ignatius Sancho, John Marrant, and Olaudah Equiano, for example. Not all did, unfortunately. Despite her unprecedented fame and notoriety, Phillis Wheatley died in obscurity and poverty. Anton Wilhelm Amo, who we think was the first Black person to earn a PhD in Europe (from the University of Wittenberg in 1734), moved back to the Gold Coast, it is suspected, after an embarrassing, racist incident thought to have been caused by an aborted romance with a white woman.[17] Jacobus Capitein, a formerly enslaved man from the Gold Coast who was similarly accomplished to Amo (he, too, successfully defended his PhD dissertation in Europe, at the University of Leiden in 1742, in which he advocated that the Bible did not oppose slavery), was embraced by Dutch antiabolitionists for obvious reasons. Like Amo, Capitein left Europe and returned to the Gold Coast, where he founded a school. Also like Amo, he ran into trouble over a love affair, in his case running afoul of church authorities.[18] Capitein seems to have fallen from Dutch grace and was buried in an unmarked grave upon his death in 1747. We can begin to understand how he was seen by his contemporaries through these words, which a fellow student at Leiden inscribed in the foreword to Capitein's dissertation: "See this Moor, his skin is black, but white his soul . . . He will bring faith, hope and love to the Africans, so they will, whitened, honour the Lamb, together with him."[19]

The small, elite group of Black intellectuals wrote very few words about the matter of their "Blackness" in a world still wrestling with who and what they *were*, and what the relation between "Blackness" and "whiteness" could possibly be in European economies defined by the massive trade in Black human beings. No matter how brilliant an individual of color might be, no matter how much fame, respect, or financial success she or he might achieve, the anti-Black racism embedded in the metaphysics of the Enlightenment meant, sadly, that even the most assimilated and acculturated Black person could unwittingly be standing on a trap door: no matter how far they rose in European society, they were always in danger of a monumental fall from grace, even in death. Thus was the curious fate of Angelo Soliman, the embodiment of unparalleled Black achievement in all of the eighteenth century.

Soliman was born around 1721, likely in Kanem-Bornu (present-day Nigeria). He was stolen from his family as a child, forced into the black box of slavery. He received the name Angelo Soliman in captivity, as his first name meant "angel," and his surname was probably a reference to the Sollima family, a prominent family in the Catholic nobility. He was sold in Italy to a noblewoman who then reportedly offered Soliman as a gift to the imperial governor of Sicily, Count Lobkowitz, who kept Soliman with him during his travels and even on the battlefield. When Lobkowitz died, Soliman ended up in Vienna in 1753 or 1754, under the control of Prince Wenzel von Liechtenstein. As Iris Wigger and Spencer Hadley write, "[h]is path from Nigeria to Europe, and ultimately to Vienna, was not only influenced by an established slave-trade network but also shaped by social connections in the aristocracy."[20]

The prince held Soliman as a servant, a so-called court moor, and dressed him in exotic styles. But the prince dismissed him when Soliman, without permission, married the aristocratic widow Magdalena Christiano, the sister of the French general François Etienne de Kellermann. Nevertheless, Soliman's stature only increased, and his black box began to crack open. He continued to move in aristocratic circles, rejoined the royal court as an educator under the prince's successor, and joined a Masonic lodge in Vienna called Zur wahren Eintracht (True Harmony), which counted Mozart and Haydn among its members. Soliman became the grand master of this lodge and changed its rituals to have a more scholarly bent, so much so that he is still celebrated in Masonic lore as Angelus Solimanus, the "Father of Pure Masonic Thought." He spoke multiple languages. He counted Austrian royalty among his dearest friends. Wigger and Hadley conclude that "Soliman was, as far as we know, the most prominent and famous black person in eighteenth-century Austria."[21] This is no doubt the case for Europe as a whole.

In death none of this mattered, only his Blackness. Soliman died on November 21, 1796. Despite the pleas of his daughter Josephine, who demanded that police hand over her father's body, Soliman would not receive a proper Christian burial. Instead, the body fell into the hands of the director of the Royal Natural History Collection, Abbé Simon Eberlé, who had hatched his heinous plan while Soliman was still alive, petitioning the government for the "cession of the corpse." What followed was unspeakable. Wigger and Hadley explain that Eberlé "ordered a death mask to be created before Soliman's skin was removed and prepared for exhibition with a stuffing compound. The so created figure was then dressed up as a 'savage' in a loin cloth, with an ostrich feather crown and glass beads, and presented to the public in the midst of taxidermised exotic animals."[22] In the ultimate humiliation, Soliman was placed on display at the museum, a debased artifact trapped behind glass, a literal realization of permanent suspension in a black box. As late as 1806, this perverse specter of European primitivism and anti-Black racism was still proudly on display. Eventually it was moved to a warehouse, which burned in the October Revolution of 1848. Angelo Soliman never received the burial worthy of his social status.

What we learn from reading the debates and exchanges analyzed in this book is that identity among a people composed of some fifty million souls is always and for everyone a black box, in that it ultimately is irreducible. At the same time, the quest for culture and individual identity is endlessly surprising, as the people within this "community" have, of necessity, had to bloom as best they could in the box in which they found themselves. It was, and it is, an argument without end, and—like all truly great arguments—a story of ceaseless creativity and reinvention, a story without which any attempt to understand America's history and culture isn't just incomplete, it is absurd. For every complex problem, H. L. Mencken famously said, there's a solution that's simple, appealing, . . . and wrong. The black box stands, in one of its many meanings, for the written engagement with and resistance against the confines of this malign construct. In its second metaphorical meaning, it stands for the ultimate irreducibility of the complexities of the human experience that have unfolded in this country since the sixteenth century through the dance of the color line. Finally, most personally and importantly for me, it stands for that square space that my good-hearted son-in-law decided to check when my granddaughter was born.

Henry Louis Gates, Jr.
Cambridge, Massachusetts
September 4, 2023

The Black Box

CHAPTER ONE

◇

Race, Reason, and Writing

We will begin this portrait of the singular poet Phillis Wheatley with a look at some numbers. By the summer of 1761, an estimated 4,498,897 enslaved Africans had been forcibly transported to the New World from Africa. Of that number, 211,227 had been brought to North America. On July 11 of that year, the slave ship *Phillis* docked in Boston, having sailed from Africa's Windward Coast, the northern border of Sierra Leone and the southern border of Liberia. Among the enslaved men, women, and children on board was a girl of about seven years old, her age estimated due to the condition of her teeth. She was but one of the 7,161 enslaved Africans who arrived in North America that year alone.[1] The young girl was sold to John Wheatley, a Boston merchant who purchased her as a gift for his wife, Susanna Wheatley. They named her Phillis, her own name a perpetual reminder of her suffering during the Middle Passage.[2]

The Wheatleys taught Phillis to read, and she quickly mastered English. By 1765 she was writing her own poetry, and in December 1767, now thirteen or fourteen, she had her first poem published in the *Newport Mercury* newspaper. An avid patriot, she commemorated the Boston Massacre with a poem in 1770. That same year she rose to prominence with her elegy "On the Death of Mr. George Whitefield," a leading British Methodist evangelical who had inspired the Great Awakening in Massachusetts. By 1772, Wheatley had written enough poems to compile a book manuscript. The Wheatleys took out advertisements in *The Censor* three times, boldly soliciting potential subscribers with their "Proposals for Printing by Subscription." Wheatley's book would consist of twenty-eight poems "put to the Press as soon as three Hundred Copies are subscribed for."[3]

Many white people, on both sides of the Atlantic, at this time would have found it difficult to believe that a Black person, to say nothing of a Black female teenager, enslaved at that, could craft such reasoned and elegant poetry. Anticipating these complaints, the Wheatleys' advertisement of February 29, 1772, emphasized that "[t]he Poems having been seen and read by the best Judges, who think them well worthy of the Public view; and upon critical examination, they find that the declared Author was capable of writing them." Wheatley's definitive biographer Vincent Carretta notes that "Proposals" was unique "because it was the first in what would soon become a tradition of having white commentators or editors attest to the authenticity of works by people of African descent."[4]

On October 28, 1772, as Joanna Brooks has convincingly argued, some of the most august members of Boston society, including John Hancock and Thomas Hutchinson, signed an attestation, still tinged with insult, to "assure the World, that the POEMS specified in the following Page, were (as we verily believe) written by PHILLIS, a young Negro Girl, who was but a few Years since, brought as an uncultivated Barbarian from *Africa*, and has ever since been, and now is, under the Disadvantage of serving as a Slave in a Family in this Town." They slightly revised the concluding language of the *Censor* advertisement, proclaiming, "She has been examined by some of the best Judges, and is thought qualified to write them."[5] Fourteen of these eighteen men had graduated from Harvard; seven were enslavers themselves.

But still, Wheatley could not entice three hundred subscribers. In 1773, still enslaved, accompanying the Wheatleys' son, she traveled to England to seek the support of Selina Hastings, Countess of Huntingdon. A reformer who would go on to organize a small group of evangelical churches in 1783, the countess was active in the antislavery movement. Hastings encouraged Wheatley and later other formerly enslaved women and men to write and publish in order to prove the argument even more forcefully that Black people were just as intelligent, just as capable of writing, as were white Europeans. Through writing, Black people could show that they were endowed with the same status as Europeans, as equally created human beings; in short, that enslaved people, too, possessed reason. Wheatley's *Poems on Various Subjects, Religious and Moral* was finally published by Archibald Bell in London in September 1773.[6]

Why was the humanity of people of African descent up for debate? Where did these ideas come from? Why did Black men and women—with the aid of "enlightened" abolitionists—have to adopt these postures to prove they were on equal footing? And why did their pursuit of this proof hinge on writing?

This enslaved teenage girl, with her gift for versification and her slim book of poems, played an outsize role in the court of Western letters. To understand the enormity of Wheatley's accomplishment—becoming probably at age nineteen the very first person of African descent to publish a book of poems in the English language—it is necessary to see it in light of that fraught history. As shocking as it sounds to us today, "scholars" of the Enlightenment raised questions about what sort of beings sub-Saharan Africans actually were. Were they members of the human community? Were Africans "reasonable" people, according to Cartesian thought? In the eighteenth century, poetry was the highest sign of civilization. It was the window onto the spirit of a people, their "national character." Blackness was constructed as a transcendent essence, not bound by geography. Could Wheatley write her sisters and brothers into the human community, into that sublime realm of "the arts and sciences," through the quality of her verse? This was the "racial mountain" whose precipice the teenage Black female poet had to climb.

Wheatley's name crowns elementary schools and women's clubs across the country. She graces the pages of innumerable anthologies. A prominent statue on Commonwealth Avenue in Boston monumentalizes her achievement. Generations of Black writers would follow in her footsteps. It is quite striking that two prominent Black feminists even saw fit not only to reimagine her life, but to literalize as an actual "trial" the events preceding the signing of the letter of attestation that prefaces her book of poems. Shirley Graham did so in 1949 (two years before she would marry W. E. B. Du Bois) in her CBS radio play, *The Story of Phillis Wheatley*, as David Waldstreicher, I believe, was the first scholar to report. More than a decade earlier, in 1932, the civil rights activist and educator Mary Church Terrell had similarly breathed life into Wheatley for a bicentennial celebration held in Washington, DC. Terrell drafted a pageant dramatizing Wheatley's life that featured a parade of notable Bostonians also "authenticating" Wheatley's poetry in the manner of an oral examination. The first scholar, as far as I am aware, to uncover Terrell's play was Lurana Donnels O'Malley, in 2018—more than eight decades after it debuted.

The actual form by which Phillis Wheatley was "critically examined"—the process that led to the curious document's signing—remains, as it has always been, a matter of speculation. Based on Terrell's drama, O'Malley writes, "several groups of eminent white authorities call upon Phyllis Wheatley to demonstrate her knowledge and skills. These authorities range from friends of Wheatley's owners, John and Susanna Wheatley, and the eighteen Boston men who sign a declaration of Wheatley's competence to the assembled guests of the Countess of Huntingdon in England."[7] Joanna Brooks theorizes that the document must have been signed before, during, or after an emergency meeting at Faneuil Hall on a colonial pay matter, where the signers would have been conveniently present. Waldstreicher points to Shirley Graham's radio play as the source of the image of an actual trial, but argues that the signers, bitter political rivals, would never

have met as a group in Wheatley's parlor or almost anywhere else, for that matter, and dismisses the idea of an
actual oral examination, collectively administered, out of
hand.[8]

That Wheatley was examined, her biographer Vincent
Carretta notes, is not in doubt. This is a fact of which we
can be certain because, with slightly different wording,
both the *Censor* advertisements and the so-called attestation say that she was; but we do not know the whole
truth—the truth of exactly *how* or *when* that examination
or series of examinations occurred. As Carretta soberly
concludes, "Wheatley's 'best Judges' examined her and her
writings between 1770 and 1773, more likely as individuals, or at most in small groups, rather than as participants
in an assembly of all the signers of the 'Attestation.'" Even
more surprising, Carretta tells us, this pernicious form of
addressing doubts about Wheatley's own authorship continued after her book appeared in print: "Following the
publication of her *Poems*, Wheatley continued to produce
compositions upon request and in front of witnesses."[9]

How any contemporary scholar could not see the demand that a Black author, in whatever form, "prove" their
own authorship as part of the relentless anti-Black racism
attendant upon the larger discourse of race and reason in
the eighteenth century would be quite difficult to understand. I've often used the word "trial" to name this offensive

ritual, for there was nothing innocent or neutral or generous about the necessity of white interlocutors demanding
that a Black author "prove" that she or he wrote her or his
own text. For me, this form of authentication was indeed a
"trial," but a figurative one. I coined the term as a trope
and in various ways—perhaps not successfully—attempted
to find a way to imagine the pressure and stress such inci-
dents of "authentication" might generate within that author, especially in 1772, when the stakes over the African's
"place in nature" were so high.

Carretta rightly recognized the intent of my use of
"an allegorical trial symbolizing the practice of requiring
white authentication of Black authorship,"[10] a practice
with a long and ugly history in the African American literary tradition that seems to have commenced with an authenticating preface to James Gronniosaw's slave narrative
published in 1772—one year before Wheatley's *Poems*
were published but the same year in which the *Censor* advertisements appeared (in February, March, and April)
and the same year in which Wheatley's statement of authentication was signed. These events established a convention of the inclusion of authenticating prefaces to
introduce the autobiographical slave narratives written
from this time through the Civil War. After the Civil
War, similar forms of authentication of Black authorship
continued through the twentieth century.[11] That two other

Black scholars before me—both women, both feminists—
had not only also seen this authentication ritual as the in-
sulting, racist ritual that it was but had chosen to dramatize
it as a literal event, to invent dialogue for the imagined
exchanges between Phillis Wheatley and her white au-
ditors and to stage it as an actual trial, underscores the
lasting power of this repeated trope within the Black tradition. (I included Shirley Graham's children's book in
the bibliography of my book, *The Trials of Phillis Wheatley*,
as it was one of a number of popular treatments of Wheatley written for young people. The first time I read it was
at Harvard's Schlesinger Library, in Graham's papers.
Imagine my delight when I learned that it included a trial
scene and that Graham had also broadcast a version of it
as a radio play!) Why would three Black scholars—there
may be others—choose to represent this vaguely defined
event, one whose historical details are indeterminate, in
the form of dramatized or imagined trials or oral examinations, constituting a kind of discourse within Wheatley
studies? This matter certainly merits further study. As
Hollis Robbins writes, "The image of gatekeeper judges
dramatizes the burden on Black writers to write themselves into the human community rather than being welcomed," and the persistence of this trope underscores that
heavy burden.[12]

In this book I will show how Black people perceived

themselves, perceived their so-called race, and put those perceptions into words. Writing and language were key in the formation of this nation within a nation. Placed on the defensive by European and American philosophers, Black people fought back in various ways, and in fighting back, they planted the seeds of a shared history, a shared culture.

White People Are from Earth, Black People Are from Mercury

Let's go back to the Renaissance, a period lousy with examples of racist dismissals of Black intellect. Bernard Le Bovier de Fontenelle, in *A Discourse of a Plurality of Worlds* (1686), musing about the inhabitants of Mercury, wrote, "I fancy they have no Memory at all, like most of the Negroes; that they make no reflexions; and what they do is by sudden starts, and perfect hap-hazard. In short, Mercury is the bedlam of the Universe."[13]

In 1773, the same year in which Phillis Wheatley's poems were published, the Bordeaux Royal Academy of Sciences solicited essays on the source of "Blackness." The authors pointed to Blackness as a result of God's plan, moral fault, climate, and even species "degeneration."[14] David Hume had written in "Of National Characters" in 1748:

I am apt to suspect the negroes and in general all other species of men (for there are four or five different kinds) to be naturally inferior to the whites. There never was a civilized nation of any other complexion than white, nor even any individual eminent either in action or speculation. No ingenious manufactures amongst them, no arts, no sciences. On the other hand, the most rude and barbarous of the whites, such as the ancient GERMANS, the present TARTARS, have still something eminent about them, in their valour, form of government, or some other particular. Such a uniform and constant difference could not happen, in so many countries and ages, if nature had not made an original distinction betwixt these breeds of men. Not to mention our colonies, there are NEGROE slaves dispersed all over EUROPE, of whom none ever discovered any symptoms of ingenuity; tho' low people, without education, will start up amongst us, and distinguish themselves in every profession. In JAMAICA, indeed, they talk of one negroe as a man of parts and learning; but 'tis likely he is admired for very slender accomplishments, like a parrot who speaks a few words plainly.[15]

The "one negroe" to whom Hume referred was Francis Williams, a free Black man from Jamaica, who was educated in the law in London, who wrote poetry in Latin, and whose work was the talk of the English capital in the

1740s. Hume knew that Black people could read and write; that they were intelligent, articulate, sophisticated, and aristocratic. But he chose to ignore the evidence, not even mentioning the great Black sixteenth-century university in Timbuktu. Consciously or unconsciously, Hume created a discourse that we might call "race and reason," which became a powerful tool in the justification of the eighteenth-century slave trade. All of the major Enlightenment thinkers who wrote about this discourse took their starting point from Hume.

In 1764, Immanuel Kant, in *Observations on the Feeling of the Beautiful and the Sublime*, wrote:

> The Negroes of Africa have by nature no feeling that rises above the trifling. . . .
> So fundamental is the difference between these two races of man, and it appears to be as great in regard to mental capacities as in color. The religion of fetishes so widespread among them is perhaps a sort of idolatry that sinks as deeply into the trifling as appears to be possible to human nature. A bird feather, a cow's horn, a conch shell, or any other common object, as soon as it becomes consecrated by a few words, is an object of veneration and of invocation in swearing oaths. The blacks are very vain but in the Negro's way, and so talkative that they must be driven apart from each other with thrashings. . . .[16]

Even antislavery philosophes such as Montesquieu and Voltaire harbored racist attitudes toward Black people. Montesquieu famously opposed slavery in *The Spirit of the Laws*, published in 1748, but his opposition to the institution did not mean he believed in racial equality. He asserted that those who live near the equator have "distended or relaxed fiber endings" and "no curiosity, no noble enterprise, no generous sentiment." Two years later, in an unpublished note, he described the free Black people living in the French Caribbean colony of Saint-Domingue as "so naturally lazy that those who are free do nothing."[17] Saint-Domingue would, of course, become the Republic of Haiti in 1804, the only nation to gain its independence as the result of a successful slave rebellion.

Voltaire, who also opposed slavery in theory, wrote in *Essay on the Spirit of Nations* (1769) that Africans were the Other of Europeans: "their round eyes, their flat noses, their invariably fat lips, the wool of their head, even the extent of their intelligence reflects prodigious divergences between them and other men."[18]

Yet Wheatley's book of poetry did the abolitionist work that it was intended to do for some skeptics. Voltaire, for example, reversed himself, writing to the Baron de Constant de Rebecque in 1774, a year after Wheatley's book was published, that "genius, which is rare everywhere, is [nonetheless] found in all climates. Fontenelle was wrong to say that there would never be poets among the Negroes: there is now a Negress who writes very good English verse."[19]

But not all skeptics were convinced, including, most notably, one of the founding fathers and a future president of the United States, Thomas Jefferson.

In his *Notes on the State of Virginia* (1785), Thomas Jefferson's "objections" to Black people were "political, . . . physical and moral." "The first difference which strikes us is that of colour," he wrote. It was a difference, he said, "fixed in nature." "And is this difference of no importance? Is it not the foundation of a greater or less share of beauty in the two races? Are not the fine mixtures of red and white, the expressions of every passion by greater or less suffusions of colour in the one, preferable to that eternal monotony, which reigns in the countenances, that immovable veil of black which covers all the emotions of the other race?" Like the other leading thinkers of the day, Jefferson traded heavily in the pseudoscience of race, postulating that what we think of as "racial difference" was more than a mere difference in skin tone, more than "skin-deep," as it were; color and other physical characteristics signified immutable differences in character, intelligence, and culture.[20]

Though less visible, the second difference, according to Jefferson, is the one between desire on one side (Black) and sentiment, sensation, and reason on the other (white). Of Black people, Jefferson wrote, "Their griefs are transient. Those numberless afflictions, which render it doubtful whether heaven has given life to us in mercy or in wrath, are less felt, and sooner forgotten with them. In general, their existence appears to participate more of sensation than reflection. To this must be ascribed their disposition to sleep when abstracted from their diversions, and unemployed in labour." In sum, according to Jefferson, "it appears to me that in memory they are equal to the whites; in reason, much inferior, as I think one could scarcely be found capable of tracing and comprehending the investigations of Euclid; and that in imagination they are dull, tasteless, and anomalous. It would be unfair to follow them to Africa for this investigation."

On the subject of art and music, Jefferson held an almost opposite view. At a most basic level, Jefferson ranked the musical ability of Black people above that of white people, praising them as "more generally gifted than the whites with accurate ears for tune or time, and they have been found capable of imagining a small catch." But, consistent with his other positions, Jefferson questioned the Black capacity for complexity: "Whether they will be equal to the composition of a more extensive run of melody, or of complicated harmony, is yet to be proved."

Judging by Jefferson's assessment of Phillis Wheatley, I suspect his conclusion would be in the negative:

> Among the blacks is misery enough, God knows, but no poetry. Love is the peculiar oestrum of the poet. Their love is ardent, but it kindles the senses only, not the imagination. Religion indeed has produced a Phyllis Whately [sic] but it could not produce a poet. The compositions published under her name are below the dignity of criticism. . . . Epictetus, Terence, and Phaedrus were slaves. But they were of the race of whites. It is not their condition then, but nature, which has produced the distinction.

In other words, race, or "nature," was at the root of artistic ability and thought—of *any* ability and thought, for that matter. Thought was the hallmark of being human, a capacity held almost exclusively by whites. Nowhere did Jefferson express more strongly his conviction that Black people were less human than their white counterparts than in his heinous assertion regarding the sexuality of African women, in which Jefferson writes of "the preference of the Oranootan for the black woman over those of his own species." One can think of these women as Phillis Wheatley's metaphorical mothers, since she claimed that she had been snatched from her parents' arms. With a vulgar swipe of his quill, Jefferson makes clear what he believes to be their true status on the great chain of being: the African rests between human and animal, in a state intermittent between those conditions. That is why Jefferson was obligated to dismiss the quality of Phillis Wheatley's poetry, to take the opposing view of Voltaire, who argued that Wheatley's work had disproven aspersions cast on the innate intelligence of Black people.

"I advance it therefore as a suspicion only," Jefferson concluded, "that the blacks, whether originally a distinct race, or made distinct by time and circumstances, are inferior to the whites in the endowments both of body and mind." Such indisputable inferiority made emancipation problematic and integration impossible. "This unfortunate difference of colour, and perhaps of faculty," Jefferson wrote, "is a powerful obstacle to the emancipation of these people. Many of their advocates, while they wish to vindicate the liberty of human nature are anxious also to preserve its dignity and beauty. . . . Among the Romans emancipation required but one effort. The slave, when made free, might mix with, without staining the blood of his master. But with us a second is necessary, unknown to history. When freed, he is to be removed beyond the reach of mixture."

Thomas Jefferson found the presence of Black people so incompatible with the ideals of America that, if freed, they must be shipped back across the Atlantic Ocean. It was Africa that stood "beyond the reach of mixture."

"Scientific Moonshine"

Today, thanks to remarkable developments in genetics research, we know that, scientifically, what we popularly call "race" is a social construct—that all human beings, no matter how different we might seem from one another based on physical traits such as hair texture, facial structure, and skin color, are more than 99 percent identical genetically. DNA testing offers us the opportunity to create a different language—beyond race—to explain not only individual origins but also our shared heritage.[21] Nevertheless, the idea that races are essences, and that people who look very different physically are members of distinct "races" that have distinct characteristics, is still a widely shared part of our common popular culture, in the United States and throughout the world. Cultural characteristics have come to be accepted as biological; as scientific, essential, and unalterable; as "natural."

This unscientific and historically dangerous conflation of character with "characteristics" was born in the eighteenth century, precisely when Europeans were attempting to justify the slave trade even in the discourse of philosophy.

Kant, who authored the essay "Of the Different Human Races," broke new ground by defining "races." According to the evolutionary anthropologist Nina Jablonski, Kant "classified people into four fixed races, which were arrayed in a hierarchy according to color and talent." He did so from a position of ignorance; Jablonski writes that "Kant had scant personal knowledge of human diversity but opined freely about the tastes and finer feelings of groups about which he knew nothing. For Kant and his many followers, the rank-ordering of races by skin color and character created a self-evident order of nature that implied that light-colored races were superior and destined to be served by the innately inferior, darker-colored ones."

Kant's ideas were perfectly timed. "A fixed natural hierarchy of human races," Jablonski tells us, "graded in value from light to dark, gained tremendous support because they reinforced popular misconceptions about dark skin being more than a physical trait. The preference for light over dark—strictly speaking, white over Black—was derived [in part] from pre-Medieval associations of white with purity and virtue, and of Black with impurity and evil."

The bottom line: "Negative associations of dark skin and human worth were now profitable"—enormously profitable. "As the transatlantic slave trade became more lucrative, the moral polarity of skin colors was accentuated to the extent that light and dark were respectively associated with human and animal, creating one of the most sinister and long-lived patterns of unfairness that the world has ever known."[22]

In the United States specifically, it's easy to see that for African Americans, the most damaging of the works of these Enlightenment philosophers were the arguments made by Thomas Jefferson about the nature of enslaved Black people (not forgetting his outrageous speculation about the sexual relations between orangutans and African women on the African continent). The reason should be self-evident: along with Benjamin Franklin, Jefferson was the American embodiment of the Enlightenment, *and* he penned the words that "all men are created equal"—which he clearly did not believe, judging by these scandalous assertions in *Notes on the State of Virginia*.

Before examining the ways that African Americans responded in print to Mr. Jefferson, creating a veritable subgenre in which they "fought back"—a fight that would persist up to the Civil War—it's essential to understand not just *how* but *why* writing became so critical in the assessment of an entire continent of people, to a so-called race's place on the great chain of being.[23]

"AFRICA, THE UNHISTORICAL, UNDEVELOPED SPIRIT"

In *The Philosophy of History*, published in 1837, G. W. F. Hegel wrote that Africa "is no historical part of the World; it has no movement or development to exhibit. . . . What we properly understand by Africa, is the Unhistorical, Undeveloped Spirit, still involved in the conditions of mere nature, and which had to be presented here only as on the threshold of the World's History."[24]

Hegel claimed—falsely—that Africa lacked a tradition of writing, either in European languages or indigenous African languages. Like Hume, he ignored the Black written tradition in Arabic at the University of Timbuktu. It didn't fit his thesis. Without writing, according to Hegel, there is no memory that is iterable, capable of being reliably repeated; and without iterable memory, there can be no meaningful history of a people. Beings are "human" because they can recount their histories; they can recount their histories because they have memory; and they can repeat and share their memories collectively through writing and through writing only. Without writing and without history, Black people in Africa existed wholly outside "the range of culture," were devoid of a sense "of a Higher Power," of respect for themselves, for others, and for the universal principles of "Justice and Morality" that in Europe and America were associated with "humanity." Prone to cannibalism, polygamy, and other uncivilized activities, their predilection for slavery—as both sellers and those sold—was, according to Hegel, the "Natural condition" of the Negro.

Very early in the history of the slave trade, at least one person made the argument in print that Africans were human beings, just like Europeans: the Reverend Morgan Godwyn. In 1680, forty-three years after Descartes wrote "I think, therefore I am" and well before the Enlightenment began, this forty-year-old Oxford graduate who had been an Anglican preacher in the colony of Virginia published the book *The Negro's and Indians Advocate*. He argued against the bizarre notion that persons of African descent were not really human beings in an effort to support his belief that Native Americans and Black people should be baptized and converted to Christianity rather than perish in their so-called savage states. Godwyn made the case that enslaved people could be baptized and still remain enslaved, an idea gleefully adopted by slaveholding planters.

How can it be, Godwyn asked, that Black Africans are not considered human when "the consideration of the shape and figure of our Negro's Bodies, their Limbs and Members; their Voice and Countenance, [are] in all things according with other Mens; and [second] together with their Risibility and Discourse [the capacity to laugh and the capacity to communicate in speech or writing, which he calls] (Man's peculiar Faculties) should be sufficient Conviction. How should they otherwise be capable of Trades, and other no less Manly imployments; as also of Reading and Writing, or show so much Discretion in management of Business . . . were they not truly Men?"[25]

Godwyn made the case for the common humanity of Black people and Europeans in terms of reason, reading, and writing—the "Three Rs," as it were. This refutation of the idea that Black people weren't fully human because they couldn't read or write, however, remained a minority view. After all, Hume and Kant were writing more than sixty years *after* Godwyn made his case.

WRITING BACK, FIGHTING BACK

Black people fought back—wrote back—against these racist ideas in part to express themselves, but also to refute racist allegations about the nature of the Negro.

In 1573, exactly two hundred years before Phillis Wheatley published her book of poetry, "El Negro" Juan Latino published *his* book of poetry, in Latin. The formerly enslaved polymath and professor is considered the first Black European poet.

Born in what is now Ghana, Anton Wilhelm Amo (1703–1769) was taken to Amsterdam as a child and later to Germany, where he became a servant in the home of Anton Ulrich, Duke of Brunswick-Wolfenbüttel. The duke sent him to fine European schools,[26] and it is believed that Amo was the first African to attend a European university. He went on to earn his PhD at Wittenberg in 1734 and two years later returned as a professor to the university at Halle, where he had studied. Following a vicious lampooning, apparently because he was in love with a white woman, he returned to Ghana in 1747, where he died a few years later.

Jacobus Capitein (1717–1747) was a contemporary of Amo's. Like Amo, he was born in the area that now corresponds to Ghana, then called the Gold Coast. Enslaved by the Dutch West India Company and taken to Holland as a boy, he was raised in The Hague in the home of a man named Jacobus Van Goch, who allowed him to pursue an education. He went to the University of Leiden in 1737 and in 1742 earned an advanced degree thanks to a dissertation that was, of all things, a defense of slavery. He returned to the land of his birth, where he became "the Black minister" at Elmina Castle, the headquarters of the Dutch slave trade on the west coast of Africa.[27]

There were countless others. Francis Williams, so reviled by David Hume, attended the University of Cambridge before returning to Jamaica to start a boys' school. Job ben Solomon wrote his way out of slavery in Maryland. Ignatius Sancho's two-volume *Letters of the Late Ignatius Sancho, an African* was published posthumously in 1782. Olaudah Equiano, the author of a slave narrative published in 1789, found fame as a writer unmatched in reputation until Frederick Douglass published his bestselling slave narrative in 1845. These people were treated as metaphorical specimens of the African rather than as actual human beings. This eighteenth-century discourse of race and reason persisted well into the next century.

The fight against that discourse persisted also. For example, the brilliant author Alexander Crummell, the hero of W. E. B. Du Bois who would become a pioneering Black abolitionist, Pan-Africanist, Episcopal priest, and educator in Liberia, wrote that the inspiration for his success was the notoriously racist senator from South Carolina John C. Calhoun. When Crummell was an errand boy in the Anti-Slavery Office in New York City in 1833 or 1834, he overheard a conversation among "the Secretary and two eminent lawyers from Boston" in which they reported that, over dinner in Washington, Calhoun had declared "[t]hat if he could find a Negro who knew the Greek syntax, he would then believe that the Negro was a human being and should be treated as a man."[28]

Crummell sought to become "that Negro." In 1853, after four years in the classical curriculum at Queens' College at the University of Cambridge, Crummell became the first African American to earn a bachelor's degree from that august institution, emerging fully fluent in Greek—all to refute John C. Calhoun's racist notion that Black people were innately inferior unless at least one of them wrote and spoke Greek.

Whether they wanted to be or not, these Black authors were engaged in—one could say trapped in, forced into—a complex act of "representing," functioning as synecdoches for the race. Frederick Douglass understood this, referring to himself as "the 'representative' of the 'black race.'"[29] Phillis Wheatley was *the Negro, the African*. One solitary and quite vulnerable individual was made to stand for, or represent, the entire group—in this case, an entire continent of human beings.

Black people fought back against the discourse of race and reason by creating their own genre of literature, which today we call the slave narratives. Again, writing was the key. Enslavers knew this. A person who could write could demand their rights and organize to do so. Writing was seen as such a powerful act that enslaved Black people were prohibited from learning how to as part of South Carolina's Negro Act of 1740, which had been passed in response to the Stono Rebellion slave uprising of the previous year. Many enslaved people who were freed or who escaped to the North equated freedom with literacy. For some of these men and women, after 1830, the road to freedom led to the lecture circuit, where speakers would follow their tours with book-length autobiographical accounts of their bondage and their freedom. Within this genre, formerly enslaved people invented their own peculiar metaphor or trope, one I term the trope of the talking book, the image of the voice speaking in the text, which is itself a metaphor for a Black person making the text of Western letters speak in their own voice.

Each of the authors of the first five Black autobiographical narratives (four slave narratives and a Black captivity and conversion narrative) employed this image in their texts: James Ukawsaw Gronniosaw in 1770; John Marrant (who was born free but lived with the Cherokee for two years) in 1785; Ottobah Cugoano in 1787; his best friend, Equiano, in 1789; and finally John Jea in 1811.[30] In the small Black literary world of London, the metaphor spread. In addition to the circulation of big ideas in a small pool, three of these authors, as Phillis Wheatley had been before them, were encouraged to write and/or had their publications subsidized by the Countess of Huntingdon, another link in the chain.

James Albert Ukawsaw Gronniosaw was born in what is now Nigeria and was sold into slavery in 1730. For more than twenty years, he lived enslaved in the home of the Dutch Reformed minister Theodorus Jacobus Frelinghuysen (Freedlandhouse in the narrative), who emancipated him upon his death. Focusing largely on his spiritual journey, Gronniosaw deployed the trope of the talking book in his book for the first time.

> [My master] used to read prayers in public to the ship's crew every Sabbath day; and when I first saw him read, I was never so surprised in my whole life as when I saw the book talk to my master; for I thought it did, as I observed him to look upon it, and move his lips. I wished it would do so to me. As soon as my master had done reading, I follow'd him to the place where he put the book, being mightily delighted with it, and when nobody saw me, I open'd it, and put my ear down close upon it, in great hope that it would say something to me; but was very sorry and greatly disappointed when I found it would not speak, this thought immediately presented itself to me, that every body and every thing despis'd me because I was Black.[31]

The trope of the talking book is the scene of education in all slave narratives in which a book "speaks" to the enslaved person. In this moment is the first step toward education, freedom, and, in a word, enlightenment. It is an allegory that refutes the anti-Black racist discourse that we saw in Hume and Kant and Jefferson. Knowing that the text will not speak to one who is enslaved, Gronniosaw makes the text speak. He makes the text contain his voice, the Black voice; he makes it reflect his face, the face of Blackness. It is a bold move, both to write and publish a book in the first place, to prove to racists that Black people possessed reason, and then to throw the whole process in their faces by creating a trope, a scene of instruction that names the act being performed. It was a brilliant gesture.

Black people also fought back by entering the discursive arena and writing back, critically, against Thomas Jefferson, as we can see in the writings of Benjamin Banneker (1731–1806), the first Black mathematician and astronomer. Banneker was freeborn. His grandmother taught him to read, and he may have been educated by Quakers. Around 1755 he built a wooden clock that lasted until his death. Between 1792 and 1797, he produced an annual almanac that was published by abolitionists in Pennsylvania.[32]

On August 19, 1791, in response to Jefferson's vile conjecture, Banneker wrote him a letter directly, in which he included an advance copy of his almanac. "I suppose it is a truth too well attested to you," Banneker wrote, "to need a proof here, that we are a race of beings, who have long labored under the abuse and censure of the world; that we have long been looked upon with an eye of contempt; and that we have long been considered rather as brutish than human, and scarcely capable of mental endowments. . . . I apprehend you will embrace every opportunity, to eradicate that train of absurd and false ideas and opinions. . . ."

We are all endowed "with the same faculties," Banneker continued, and "however diversified in situation or color, we are all of the same family." He threw Jefferson's own words at him, citing the opening words of the Declaration of Independence. "But, Sir," Banneker wrote, "how pitiable is it to reflect, that although you were so fully convinced of the benevolence of the Father of Mankind, and of his equal and impartial distribution of these rights and privileges, which he hath conferred upon them, that you should at the same time counteract his mercies, in detaining by fraud and violence so numerous a part of my brethren, under groaning captivity and cruel oppression, that you should at the same time be found guilty of that most criminal act, which you professedly detested in others, with respect to yourselves."[33]

Would Banneker's achievements be enough to convince Jefferson that he had been wrong all along about the nature of the Negro? Remember, Hume had said that the

Black person, in order to be equal, had to prove herself or himself in both "the arts *and* the sciences." Jefferson's response to Banneker indicated that he was willing to be shown the error of his ways. "No body wishes more than I do," he replied, "to see such proofs as you exhibit, that nature has given to our black brethren talents equal to those of the other colors of men; and that the appearance of the want of them, is owing merely to the degraded condition of their existence, both in Africa and America."

But in a letter to his friend Joel Barlow, dated October 8, 1809, Jefferson showed himself to be far less charitable: "We know he had spherical trigonometry enough to make almanacs, but not without the suspicion of aid from [Major Andrew Ellicot, who surveyed the original borders of Washington, DC, and] who was his neighbor and friend, and never missed an opportunity of puffing him. I have a long letter from Banneker, which shows him to have had a mind of very common stature indeed."

Jefferson was not to be swayed. He reduced and delimited the accomplishments of Benjamin Banneker in the realms of science and math exactly as he had dismissed the achievements of Phillis Wheatley in the realm of poetry.

WALKER'S *APPEAL*

The years between 1809, the end of Thomas Jefferson's presidency, and 1830, approximately when the abolitionist movement as we know it today and the Underground Railroad were born, were a time of tremendous transition in America. In 1793, Eli Whitney's invention of the cotton gin, or engine, revolutionized America's economy, transforming plantation-based slavery into a far more efficient and lucrative business for the owner class. For the enslaved, an already backbreaking task became more so. Before 1793, one enslaved person could clean one pound of raw cotton per day, working for fourteen hours. After 1793, the amount of product skyrocketed, with one person now able to clean fifty pounds of raw cotton in a day. The economy of the South exploded: in 1815, 200,000 bales of cotton were harvested; in 1840, that number rose to 1.35 million bales; in 1846, 2.85 million; and in 1860, 4.8 million. The transformation of the South's economy was felt the world over, with the United States supplying the vast majority of the cotton consumed in Great Britain, France, Germany, and Russia by 1860—all on the backs of enslaved African Americans.[34]

As the economy was growing, David Walker published his *Appeal to the Coloured Citizens of the World* (1829), one of the most dramatic and important examples of writing back. A tailor in Boston, Walker sewed copies of his book into suits so that free Black sailors could distribute them among the Black people enslaved in the South. The state of Georgia put a bounty on Walker's head: ten thousand dollars if he were turned over alive; a thousand if dead. He died mysteriously in 1830.

Walker's *Appeal* has four principal points, or articles, plus a preamble. Walker began by quoting Jefferson's Declaration of Independence, to refute the claims that Jefferson himself made about Blacks in his *Notes on the State of Virginia*: "unless we try to refute Mr. Jefferson's arguments respecting us," he declared, "we will only establish them."[35]

Second, Walker maintained that Black people themselves must establish a literature, a discourse, that refutes pro-slavery arguments: "For let no one of us suppose that the refutations which have been written by our white friends are enough—they are *whites*—we are *blacks*. We, and the world wish to see the charges of Mr. Jefferson refuted by the blacks *themselves*, according to their chance. . . . [O]ur oppression ought not to hinder us from acquiring all [of the learning and knowledge] we can," for one day, when freedom belongs to all Black people, "then we will want all the learning and talents among ourselves, and perhaps more, to govern ourselves."

"'Every dog must have its day,'" he wrote, and "the American's is coming to an end."

Third, Walker argued that the most insidious aspect of the Jeffersonian justification of slavery is that Africans are defined as brutes and animals. Not even the Egyptians (who, he noted, as Frederick Douglass would also, "were Africans or coloured people") "heaped the *insupportable insult* upon the children of Israel, by telling them that they were not of the *human family.*" Humanity—or lack thereof—lies at the crux of the entire argument for slavery, he said. "Can the whites deny this charge? Have they not, after having reduced us to the deplorable condition of slaves under their feet, held us up as descending originally from the tribes of *Monkeys* or *Orang-Outangs?* . . . [I]s not this insupportable?"

Finally, Walker asserted, Black people do not want to be white, but rather to be Black and free. He was determined to refute allegations of innate or biological differences between white and Black people, arguing against those who claimed that "nature herself" would have it this way. In his *Appeal*, Walker was calling out the dark side of the Enlightenment. His words were so intolerable to his white counterparts that some of his contemporaries thought his scathing indictments got him killed.

"THE REPRESENTATIVE MAN OF HIS RACE"[36]

Frederick Douglass, without a doubt, was the most famous Black person in the world after 1845, when he published his first slave narrative. He would go on to edit his own newspaper, be the leading Black figure in the abolitionist movement, become a friend of Abraham Lincoln's, serve as the US minister (ambassador) to Haiti, and live a long, prosperous, and celebrated life. The most photographed American of the nineteenth century died in 1895. This was the same year that W. E. B. Du Bois became the first Black person to earn a PhD from Harvard University, the same year that Booker T. Washington delivered his (in)famous address at the Cotton States and International Expo in Atlanta.

On July 12, 1854—a full century after Hume published his notorious footnote about "no arts, no sciences" in Africa—Douglass became the first Black person to deliver a commencement oration before a white audience, presenting the essay "The Claims of the Negro, Ethnologically Considered" at Western Reserve College, now Case Western Reserve University, in Cleveland.[37]

Douglass began with a long quote from an editorial that had recently been published in a southern newspaper,

The Richmond Examiner. The editorial laid out the issues at the heart of the justification of slavery, from the outset echoing the same argument that Jefferson had made about classical Greece's and Rome's white-skinned enslaved persons and their capacity to become free.

> The white peasant is free, and if he is a man of will and intellect, can rise in the scale of society; or at least his offspring may. He is not deprived by law of those "inalienable rights," "liberty and the pursuit of happiness," by the use of it. But here is the essence of slavery—that we do declare the negro destitute of these powers. We bind him by law to the condition of the laboring peasant for ever, without his consent, and we bind his posterity after him. Now, the true question is, have we a right to do this? If we have not, all discussions about his comfortable situation, and the actual condition of free laborers elsewhere, are quite beside the point. If the negro has the same right to his liberty and the pursuit of his own happiness that the White man has, then we commit the greatest wrong and robbery to hold him a slave—an act at which the sentiment of justice must revolt in every heart—and negro slavery is an institution which that sentiment must sooner or later blot from the face of the earth.

Douglass answered his own question regarding the right to keep Black people enslaved in perpetuity: "the

Examiner boldly asserts that the negro has no such right—
BECAUSE HE IS NOT A MAN!"

Douglass deconstructed this argument by attacking
the ranking of the human races and, more specifically,
those who thought that Africans are related more closely
to apes than to other human beings. But to do so, he, like
David Walker, had to dismiss any theory that human
beings evolved from monkeys or apes as total rubbish.
Douglass wrote:

> Common sense itself is scarcely needed to detect
> the absence of manhood in a monkey, or to recog-
> nize its presence in a negro. His speech, his reason,
> his power to acquire and to retain knowledge, . . .
> plant between him and the brute creation, a dis-
> tinction as eternal as it is palpable. Away, there-
> fore, with all the scientific moonshine that would
> connect men with monkeys; that would have the
> world believe that humanity, instead of resting
> on its own characteristic pedestal—gloriously
> independent—is a sort of sliding scale, making
> one extreme brother to the ourang-ou-tang, and
> the other to angels, and all the rest intermediaries!

He is referring, of course, to the great chain of being.
He continued:

> [T]he whole argument in defence of slavery be-
> comes utterly worthless the moment the African

is proved to be equally a man with the Anglo-Saxon. . . . Pride and selfishness, combined with mental power, never want for a theory to justify them—and when men oppress their fellow-men, the oppressor ever finds, in the character of the oppressed, a full justification for his oppression. Ignorance and depravity, and the inability to rise from degradation to civilization and respectability, are the most usual allegations against the oppressed. The evils most fostered by slavery and oppression, are precisely those which slaveholders and oppressors would transfer from their system to the inherent character of their victims. Thus the very crimes of slavery become slavery's best defence. By making the enslaved a character fit only for slavery, they excuse themselves for refusing to make the slave a freeman.

Douglass knew that to win this argument—he and all of the Black writers against Hume, Kant, Jefferson, and Hegel, and what we might think of as the popular American cultural imagination—was to prove that there *was*, in fact, a great civilization that once had thrived on the African continent, a civilization created by Black women and men. He started with the pyramids. "Egypt," he argued, "is in Africa. Pity that it had not been in Europe, or in Asia, or better still, in America! Another unhappy circumstance is, that the ancient Egyptians were not white people; but were, undoubtedly, just about as dark in complexion as many in this country who are considered genuine negroes; and that is not all," he said, referencing directly Jefferson's claims about the inherent superior beauty of the European complexion and texture of hair, "their hair was far from being of that graceful lankness which adorns the fair Anglo-Saxon head." Since Egypt was in Africa and its accomplished people were not white, Douglass concluded, Egypt alone disproved the aspersions cast upon the nature of the Negro people, and therefore, Douglass surmised, slavery itself was responsible for the degraded position of the New World people of African descent. Douglass demanded that white people admit that they had invented outrageous notions about Black peoples to justify exploiting their labor to create the most prosperous economy on earth. End slavery and racial prejudice, he said with finality, and you will see the Black man rise to the former glories of his ancestors.

When challenged to prove their common humanity with Europeans by the greatest thinkers in the Enlightenment in Europe, when they had to disprove the scandalous assertion that Black people were animals and not human beings, Black women and Black men—all formerly enslaved, or the sons and daughters of those who had been—met that challenge head-on. They sat at their desks and read and wrote books, and by doing so, they wrote themselves and their fellow persons of African descent into the human community. This focus on writing and language begged another question: What should we call the race?

◇

What's in a Name?

I was still in high school when Negroes became Black
people in the middle of the 1960s. When I applied to Yale
in 1969, on my personal statement, I wrote, "My grandfather was colored, my father is a Negro, and I am Black!"
The person probably most responsible for this transformation, after Malcolm X, was Stokely Carmichael, the char-
ismatic head of the Student Nonviolent Coordinating
Committee. Carmichael enunciated the political philosophy of Black Power during the James Meredith "March
Against Fear" on June 16, 1966, in Greenwood, Mississippi. We were Black pretty much across the board for those
two decades, until about 1988, when Jesse Jackson declared
at a press conference that we were African Americans now.[1]
Most of us have been African Americans since that time.

Three years after I first saw that Stokely Carmichael speech, I picked up *The New York Times* and read a cartoon that lampooned the name changes: Blacks, which replaced Afro-Americans, which replaced Negroes, which replaced colored people, which replaced darkies, which replaced Blacks. Had we merely traced a circle in our "revolutionary" naming practices?

Freedom for their enslaved brethren was a primary concern of the complexly structured free Negro community, in both the North and South. These men and women also longed for and fought with white citizens for equal rights for themselves. But another issue ranked high in importance. For some, it bordered on what can only be called obsession: the subject of naming; namely, what would they call themselves as a group?

This quandary over naming turned on the nineteenth-century relationship to Africa. A century earlier, both Anton Wilhelm Amo and Phillis Wheatley were called "African" and referred to themselves as such. Many Black institutions formed at that time included "African" in their name, such as the African Methodist Episcopal Church. But that was an eighteenth-century institution; by the 1830s, many Black people in America had never called Africa home. How did they feel about christening their American institutions, and themselves as a group, with the name of a now-distant land? The naming business occupied a prominent place in the minds (and writing) of free Negroes and has continued to play an important role in Black politics.

James McCune Smith, the best-educated Black man alive at the time—he earned three degrees, including an MD from the University of Glasgow in Scotland, the first person of African descent to do so—wrote an essay on Thomas Jefferson's *Notes on the State of Virginia* in 1859. The same year that John Brown was trying to launch a revolution at the arsenal in Harpers Ferry, Virginia, marked the seventy-fifth anniversary of the publication of Jefferson's infamous essay.[2] Three-quarters of a century: that proves not only the power of Jefferson's argument for those who agreed with it but the power to wound, to cast aspersions on the image of the Negro, a power so large, so irresistible, that the world's best-educated Black man saw fit to write about it in 1859, just as Frederick Douglass had five years before.

Near the end of his essay, McCune Smith noted that a crucial name change had occurred among Black people. They had set aside the words "Black" and "Negro," now opting for a new and revolutionary word: "colored."

You may have observed that we use the word "black," as distinguishing the class whom we have under consideration. This word "black," and the other word "negro," were the common, the usual, term for this class at the time Mr. Jefferson wrote. That is more than fifty years ago. The newspapers, sure indices of public opinion, NOW call this same class "colored people." The class is the same, the name is changed; they are no longer blacks, bordering on bestiality; they are "colored," and they are a "people." I will not stop to enquire whether the word "colored," be used as a euphony for black, nor whether it marks the fact of an already perceptible change in the hue of the skin of this class. It answers our argument if it shows, and it does show, a lessening of the distance—a step towards harmony and reciprocal kindness between man and his fellow man—between the black and the white man in this Republic. . . .

Then there is that other word, "people." What does it mean? Tell us poor, cringing sycophant, thou who art fearful that the two races can only live together as master and slave, what does this word "people" mean? . . . It meant men who were part of and parcel of—were the great sires and the great inheritors of this great country.[3]

In 1859, McCune Smith was merely summarizing what had already been a long and heated debate in the Black tradition for decades, going back at least to 1828 and raging in the popular press from this time to 1845, when Frederick Douglass published his slave narrative.

"Our Claims Are on America"

By 1820, due in large part to the abolition of the slave trade twelve years earlier, most of the African American population had been born in the United States. The idea of a wholesale return to Africa had lost the appeal that it had for free Black people in the first decade and a half of the nineteenth century. No one articulated this more clearly than a man named Thomas L. Jennings, a successful tailor in New York City, writing in *Freedom's Journal* in 1828:

> Our claims are on America; it is the land that gave us birth. We know no other country. It is a land in which our fathers have suffered and toiled. They have watered it with their tears and fanned it with their sighs. . . .
>
> Our relation with Africa is the same as the white man's is with Europe. We have passed through several generations in this country and consequently we have become naturalized. Our habits, our manners, our passions, our dispositions have become the same. The same mother's milk has

nourished us both in infancy; the white child and the colored have both hung on the same breast. I might as well tell the white man about England, France or Spain, the country from whence his forefathers emigrated, and call him a European, as for him to call us African.

Africa is as foreign to us as Europe is to them.[4]

The historian Dorothy Sterling tells us that antipathy toward migration to Africa was related to Black people's overarching opposition to the American Colonization Society, a white organization that advocated for and sponsored the "repatriation" of freed and formerly enslaved Black people to Africa and had established the country of Liberia in 1821. "Black public opinion in the North," Sterling writes, "now looked on the society as an enemy and branded the men who emigrated to Liberia as traitors."[5]

Debates over emigration had a long history, and support or opposition to emigration did not always divide along straight lines. Take, for instance, the first Black Freemason lodge, founded in Boston, which would later be renamed after its founder, Prince Hall. In March 1775, he and fourteen other African Americans were initiated into Freemasonry through an Irish military group stationed in Massachusetts, as no white American Masons would allow them to join. On July 3, 1775, a year and a day before the founding of the new nation, they organized African Lodge No. 1. The lodge had to get an official charter through the British after the Revolutionary War had already ended.

Nevertheless, in 1786, Hall and his compatriots wrote to Governor James Bowdoin offering support in suppressing Shays's Rebellion, seemingly indicating their commitment to the American experiment.[6]

At the same time, in the words of the scholar Chernoh Sesay, Hall "always considered, in simultaneity, multiple and seemingly controversial agendas." To wit, one year later, in 1787, Hall and more than seventy supporters pledged support for African emigration, even asking the Massachusetts General Court to support their plan. To the south in Rhode Island, the African Union Society, founded in 1780, pursued similar goals. In 1787 the society's president, Anthony Taylor, asked the federal government for help. "Our earnest desire of returning to Africa and settling there has induced us further to trouble you in order to convey a more particular idea of our proposal," he wrote. "That a number of men from among ourselves shall be sent to Africa to see if they can obtain, by gift or purchase, lands sufficient to settle upon. And if such land can be obtained, then some of these men shall return and bring information. The company then shall go without their wives and children, to make preparation for their families. This plan is agreeable to us. But as we are unable to prosecute it for want of money, this is the only reason of our troubling our superiors for assistance."[7]

The movement of free Negroes wishing to move back to Africa intensified under the leadership of Paul Cuffee (1759–1817), who would become known as the father of the "Back to Africa" movement. He was born on Cutty-hunk Island, off southern Massachusetts, one of ten children of Ruth Moses, a Wampanoag Native American, and Kofi Slocum, who had been formerly enslaved. Kofi Slocum would anglicize his first name to Cuffee, shortened to Cuff.[8]

In 1766, the Slocums bought a 116-acre farm in Dartmouth, Massachusetts, on Buzzards Bay. In 1772, Cuff Slocum died, leaving the farm to Paul and his brother John, both of whom adopted their father's first name as their surname. The farm remained in both brothers' possession for many years, but young Paul left the land behind for the sea, working on Atlantic whalers as an adolescent. The profession of whaling was so dangerous that it was open to men of any race. Paul Cuffee later became involved in maritime trading and found quick financial success.[9]

At home in Massachusetts, Paul Cuffee protested discrimination. In 1780 Paul and John and five other Black men in Dartmouth filed a petition with the state legislature protesting taxation without representation, particularly since Black people had fought for the revolution: "We apprehend ourselves to be aggrieved, in that while we are not allowed the privilege of freemen of the state, having no vote or influence in the election of those that tax us, yet many of our color (as is well known) have cheerfully entered the field of battle in the defense of the common cause, and that (as we conceive) against a similar exertion of power (in regard to taxation) too well known to need a recital in this place." Paul Cuffee was briefly jailed but succeeded in getting his taxes reduced.[10]

Two years later, he married Alice Pequit, a Pequot Indian from Martha's Vineyard. They had seven children and even built a school to ensure that racial discrimination would not deny their children and others a formal education. They owned a grist mill and a store, and, most important of all, they bought and built ships, which they used to establish a maritime business that covered the East Coast of the United States and traded with Caribbean and European nations. Paul Cuffee became the richest Black man in America, and in 1813, he became the first Black man, other than an enslaved person, to set foot in the White House. James Madison, an enslaver himself, was president at the time.[11]

In 1811, Paul Cuffee made two trips to Sierra Leone. Since 1787, British philanthropists had been trying to build a colony of free Black people there. They founded Freetown in 1792, and Sierra Leone became a colony in 1808. Cuffee became what we call an emigrationist, one of the numerous people who wanted the formerly enslaved African Americans to leave the United States for good and establish their own country in Africa—never mind what the Africans living there thought.

After his second visit, Cuffee founded the Friendly Society of Sierra Leone to encourage emigration and colonization. On December 10, 1815, he sailed for Africa's west coast with a commercial cargo and thirty-eight African Americans ranging in age from six months to sixty years; twenty of the group were children. They arrived on February 3, 1816. This was the first Black-initiated Back to Africa effort in the history of the United States.[12]

Five years later, in 1821, the American Colonization Society established the country of Liberia. Many Black people saw the ACS as racist rather than liberating. In the starkest terms, going back to Africa meant a reversal of the Middle Passage, and a vanishingly small number of Black people made the journey. According to the historian James T. Campbell, eleven hundred former Black Loyalists were settled by the British in Sierra Leone in 1792. The American Colonization Society repatriated approximately fifteen thousand free Black settlers to Liberia after 1820, and another twenty-five hundred African Americans returned to Africa between the end of the Civil War and the turn of the century.[13]

Fewer than twenty thousand African Americans voluntarily shipped themselves back to Africa. In comparison, historians estimate that about twenty-five thousand enslaved people were able to escape to the North on the Underground Railroad. Both of these figures represent a tiny percentage of the African American community. Most Black people could never break the bonds of slavery.

THE COLONIZATION DEBATES

Initially, the idea of colonization was quite popular among Black intellectuals. But they would change their minds.

Take, for instance, Paul Cuffee's best friend, James Forten of Philadelphia, another wealthy Black businessman. Initially, he shared Cuffee's Back to Africa philosophy, but in 1817 he wrote to Cuffee to tell him about an ominous meeting at Richard Allen's Mother Bethel African Methodist Episcopal Church in Philadelphia. "Three thousand at least attended," Forten wrote, "and there was not one sole [*sic*] that was in favour of going to Africa. They think that the slaveholders want to get rid of them so as to make their property more secure." The meeting resulted in a formal resolution: "Whereas our ancestors (not of choice) were the first successful cultivators of the wilds in America, we their descendents feel ourselves entitled to participate in the blessings of her luxuriant soil. . . . Resolved, that we will never separate ourselves voluntarily from the slave population in this country; they are our brethren by the ties of consanguinity, of suffering, and of wrong."[14]

This was the key: free Black people in the North believed themselves linked with their enslaved brothers and sisters to the South. As long as slavery existed, they could not consider themselves truly free.

Paul Cuffee died on September 7, 1817, and by the following year Forten had rejected colonization altogether. On December 10, 1818, Forten and Russell Parrott, the head of Philadelphia's African Literary Society, delivered an address in Philadelphia against colonization in general and against the American Colonization Society in particular. Colonization, they argued, would make life worse for the enslaved people who could not leave. "The southern masters will colonize only those whom it may be dangerous to keep among them." African Americans increasingly viewed this fact as the true motive behind the work of the ACS.

Part of their argument would not age well, that "the ultimate and final abolition of slavery" was "proceeding," seemingly inevitably. Even so, colonization was wrong in their eyes because it separated formerly enslaved people from their families and friends. "All of the heartrending agonies," the men wrote, "which were endured by our forefathers when they were dragged into bondage from Africa will again be renewed, and with increased anguish. The shores of America will, like the sands of Africa, be watered by the tears of those who will be left behind. Those who shall be carried away will roam childless, widowed, and alone, over the burning plains of Guinea."

Forten and Parrott also believed that formerly enslaved people needed the guidance of educated northerners such as themselves, who understood the importance of respectability and moral education. "Unprepared by education and a knowledge of the truths of our blessed religion for their new situation," they wrote, "those who will thus become colonists will themselves be surrounded by every suffering which can afflict the members of the human family." "The cords," they said, "which now connect them with us, will be stretched by the distance to which their ends will be carried, until they break; and all the sources of happiness, which affection and connexion and blood bestow, will be ours and theirs no more."[15]

In 1831, Forten wrote to William Lloyd Garrison, who had just launched the antislavery weekly *The Liberator*:

> I am greatly astonished that the ministers of the gospel should take so active a part in endeavoring

to convey freemen of color to Africa. Instead of doing this, they should endeavor to remove prejudice, improve the condition of the colored people by education and by having their children placed in a situation to learn a trade.

I have never conversed with an intelligent man of color (not swayed by sinister motives) who was not decidedly opposed to leaving his home for the fatal clime of Africa. I am well acquainted with all the masters of vessels belonging to this port who have been to the coast of Africa. They all agree in representing it as one of the most unhealthy countries. . . . We ask not their aid in assisting us to emigrate to Africa. We are contented in the land that gave us birth and for which many of our fathers fought and died.[16]

Black opposition to the American Colonization Society coalesced over the following decade, but the question of colonization in general did not go away. As the 1820s came to an end, free Black leaders in the North faced myriad problems with no obvious answers, problems that called into question their freedom itself. Despite the promises of the American Revolution and its emphasis on liberty and freedom, they faced discrimination from white people in all parts of their lives, regardless of their educations or incomes. As their populations grew, white resistance grew as well. They had no representation in

Congress, no national body to represent them or their interests. Their legal freedom was insecure. They stood on uncertain ground. Were they Africans, Americans, both, or neither? How could they get the security they wanted for themselves and their people?

THE BLACK CONVENTION MOVEMENT

One response was the Black Convention Movement, which began after three days of white violence in Cincinnati. The city's Black population skyrocketed during the 1820s, and by decade's end about 10 percent of its residents were Black. White people in Cincinnati viewed African Americans as competitors who took their jobs and drove down wages. City leaders turned to Ohio's decades-old "Black laws," established in 1804 and 1807, to assert their control. The laws were designed to stop Black migration into the state. They stipulated that African American migrants not only had to prove that they were free but also had to post a bond of five hundred dollars, money they would lose if they broke any law.[17]

In 1829, city leaders began to enforce these dormant laws. Black people, a great many of whom had moved to Cincinnati from other parts of the country, recognized that they were vulnerable. Most could not afford to post a five-hundred-dollar bond. They petitioned for delay of enforcement.[18]

About three hundred white men refused to wait for a judge's decision. They chose vigilantism instead. On August 15, the mob began a three-day siege of the city's Black district, known as Bucktown. The historian Carter G. Woodson later wrote that "police were unable or unwilling to restore order." Two people died, one Black and one white; many more were injured; and Bucktown suffered severe property damage.

The violence had national implications as far as determining how free the free states were in reality. Black people questioned whether they could live safely in Cincinnati or anywhere else in the North. At least one thousand African Americans decided the answer was no and fled their city and their country not for Africa, but for Canada.[19]

The convention movement was a direct response to the violence in Cincinnati, but it also reflected recent movements among free Black Americans trying to forge an activist community, such as the founding of *Freedom's Journal* and the publication of Walker's *Appeal*.[20] As the Princeton University scholar Eddie S. Glaude, Jr., puts it, the Black Convention Movement emerged "between the racial terror of Jacksonian mobs and the expressed desire to 'do something' about the circumstances of free Blacks in the North."[21] The conventions were among the most influential, varied, and lasting Black political and social networks of the nineteenth century.

Emigration, abolitionism, education, moral reform, legal equality—all were fair game for discussion at the conventions. There were national and state conventions in the Northeast; nearly seven hundred people attended conventions in New York between 1843 and 1864, and conventions picked up again after the Civil War. African Americans held state-level conventions in western states including Indiana, Illinois, Kansas, and Ohio, which served as a training ground for the great abolitionist and future diplomat and congressman John Mercer Langston. Conventions occurred in California before and after the Civil War. The Canadian cities of Drummondville (today Niagara Falls), Chatham, Amherstburg, and Toronto hosted a total of 142 delegates at four conventions between 1847 and 1858. In 1852 African Americans in Baltimore, in the slave state of Maryland, attempted to hold a convention, but a white mob attacked it on its first day. Nevertheless, the convention went on, the primary topic being emigration to Liberia.[22]

Convention delegates adopted formal proceedings that were hardly different from those of a white political convention. The events featured an opening address, usually from the person named president of the convention. There was a roll call of delegates and other significant attendees. Committees created rules and investigated important subjects or problems. There was usually a "conventional address" to summarize the convention and mobilize attendees for future work. As we shall see, speeches were sometimes deemed too controversial to be included in the minutes.[23]

In these ways, Black conventions allowed African Americans to continue what P. Gabrielle Foreman calls "an ongoing political practice, a parallel politics, actualized in the face of official exclusion, derision, and violence."[24] As one proponent of the conventions wrote in *The Colored American*, "Indeed we have no other way of proving that we have political talents."[25] Since the conventions revolved around democratic debate, delegates often came to very different conclusions. To the historian Howard Holman Bell, writing in 1953, that was the point. Reading about the debates and speeches from the conventions, he argues, "the public became indoctrinated on the issues involved. And if one convention served at cross-purposes to another, general progress was yet encouraged because the public was thus informed on all aspects of a given problem." This is an important point, as traveling to a convention required time and money, neither of which most free Black people had in excess. Indeed, the historian Jim Casey has found that while more than two thousand people attended national and state conventions before the end of the Civil War, "only 20 percent of delegates ever attended more than one convention."[26] Glaude argues that the inaugural convention of 1830, held in the aftermath of the Cincinnati violence, "was, to some extent, the first national forum for civic activity among northern free Blacks in the United States."[27]

The Baltimore activist Hezekiah Grice, a cofounder of the Legal Rights Association with William Watkins and James Deaver, was important in organizing the inaugural convention. Freeborn and educated, Grice worked as an agent for *Freedom's Journal* and became close to the abolitionists Benjamin Lundy and William Lloyd Garrison. By 1830 he had even created a map of Canada that highlighted where emigrating African Americans might live. Grice discussed a national convention with Black leaders in New York and Philadelphia. The New York contingent had already been considering a convention and believed they should host this one. In fact, an African American from Cincinnati gave an address on the topic in New York City on July 7. But that honor fell to the legendary AME Bishop Richard Allen of Philadelphia. As his biographer Richard Newman writes, Allen "maneuvered the first Black convention to be held in Philadelphia rather than let New York City's or Baltimore's Black reformers claim the honor of hosting the event."[28]

Forty delegates from seven states met at Allen's Mother Bethel AME Church. Delegates were overwhelmingly northeastern, with nearly half of them coming from Pennsylvania, and all were male.[29] Notable delegates included William Whipper, a Pennsylvania businessman and abolitionist; Austin Steward, who escaped slavery around 1815, helped fugitives flee to Canada, and owned a general store in Rochester; and the abolitionist Abraham D. Shadd of Delaware.[30]

The convention chose for its name "The American Society of Free Persons of Colour, for improving their condition in the United States; for purchasing lands; and for the establishment of a settlement in Upper Canada." It would focus on emigration, though not to Africa, and not with the assistance of the American Colonization Society. In his "Address to the Free People of Colour of these United States," Richard Allen said, "However great the debt which these United States may owe to injured Africa and however unjustly her sons have been made to bleed, and her daughters to drink of the cup of affliction, still we who have been born and nurtured on this soil, we, whose habits, manners, and customs are the same in common with other Americans, can never consent to take our lives in our hands, and be the bearers of the redress offered by that Society to that much afflicted country."[31]

With Africa out of the question, delegates proposed a

new settlement in "Upper Canada," the lands north of the
Great Lakes where Loyalists had migrated after the American Revolution, where land was inexpensive and available
and the climate familiar. Allen further argued, wrongly,
it turned out, that "the laws and prejudices of society will
have no effect in retarding their advancement to the summit of civil and religious improvement. There the diligent
student will have ample opportunity to reap the reward
due to industry and perseverance; whilst those of moder-
ate attainments, if properly nurtured, may be enabled to
take their stand as men in the several offices and situa-
tions necessary to promote union, peace, order and tran-
quility." The Black Loyalists who relocated to Nova Scotia
after the American Revolution had already found out that
Canada was hardly the promised land.

Allen died on March 26, 1831, leaving an indelible
legacy but also a power vacuum in the convention movement. Delegates met again from June 6 to 11, 1831, in
Philadelphia at what they called the First Annual Convention of the People of Colour. Along with discussions of
emigration, delegates emphasized moral suasion and "Education, Temperance and Economy." Convention leaders
invited several prominent white abolitionists to speak, including the Reverend Simeon S. Jocelyn of New Haven,
Arthur Tappan of New York, and William Lloyd Garrison
of Boston. They presented a plan for a manual labor school

that "cannot but elevate the general character of the coloured population." They proposed its location be in the "healthy and beautiful" city of New Haven, which had friendly people, fair laws, inexpensive housing, a connection to the West Indian trade, and a "literary and scientific character." The Reverend Samuel E. Cornish was named general agent of the school endeavor. He had recently tried to revive *Freedom's Journal*, which he had left in 1827. The paper had folded in 1829, in large part because of the editor and reformer John Russwurm's embrace of emigration to Africa. Cornish's new paper, *The Rights of All*, ended within a year.[32]

The 1831 convention charged the American Colonization Society with

> pursuing the direct road to perpetuate slavery, with all its unchristianlike concomitants, in this boasted land of freedom; and, as citizens and men whose best blood is sapped to gain popularity for that Institution, we would, in the most feeling manner, beg of them to desist: or, if we must be sacrificed to their philanthrophy [*sic*], we would rather die at home. Many of our fathers, and some of us, have fought and bled for the liberty, independence, and peace which you now enjoy; and, surely, it would be ungenerous and unfeeling in you to deny us an humble and quiet grave in that country which gave us birth![33]

Emigration to Canada was more enticing. The convention announced that two thousand Black Americans had moved there, and they had built two hundred houses on eight hundred acres of land, "the foundation for a structure which promises to prove an asylum for the coloured population of these United States."

This optimism marked the high point for support for emigration to Canada. The convention in Philadelphia, held from June 4 to 13, 1832, convened a committee of seven men to determine the feasibility of emigration. It consisted of William Whipper, Robert Cowley (Maryland), Thomas Coxsin (New Jersey), William Hamilton (New York), and three Pennsylvanians: John Peck, Benjamin Paschal, and J. C. Morel.[34] The committee addressed three questions in particular: Should African Americans leave the United States? If so, should they choose to move to Upper Canada? Finally, "Is there any certainty that the people of color will be compelled by oppressive legislative enactments to abandon the land of their birth for a home in a distant region?"

That home in a distant region was not without obstacles. Early scouts to Canada had "returned with a favorable report, except that citizens of these United States could not purchase lands in Upper Canada and legally transfer the same to other individuals." They also learned of white resistance, that "a part of the white inhabitants of said province had, through prejudice and the fear of being overburdened with an ejected population, petitioned the provincial parliament to prohibit the general influx of colored population from entering their limits, which threw some consternation on the prospect."

The committee argued that Black emigration from the United States would cripple efforts to help or protect those who stayed, by choice or by force, without any guarantee that it would help those who left. Importantly, it argued that sympathetic philanthropists would lose interest. They "might now rest from their labors, and have the painful feeling of transmitting to future generations, that an oppressed people, in the land of their birth, supported by the genuine philanthropists of the age, amidst friends, companions, and their natural attachments, a genial clime, a fruitful soil—amidst the rays of as proud institutions as ever graced the most favored spot that has ever received the glorious rays of a meridian sun—have abandoned their homes on account of their persecutions, for a home almost similarly precarious, for an abiding place among strangers!"

Not that life in the northern United States was much better. The committee decided against establishing a school in New Haven. It was by now a familiar story: because of "some hostility manifested by some of the inhabitants of

New Haven, against the location of the establishment in that place, it became prudent to alter the address, so as to read 'New Haven or elsewhere.'" Just as Nat Turner's rebellion of August 21 to 23, 1831, had led white legislators to pass stringent antiliteracy laws in Virginia, it had also convinced white people in New Haven of the dangers of Black education.

Emigration was off the table at the national convention in Philadelphia, held from June 3 to 13, 1833. Since "there is not now, and probably never will be actual necessity for a large emigration of the present race of free coloured people," the focus shifted to education, poverty, and moral reform at home.

"WE SHALL BE CALLED CITIZENS OF THE *UNITED STATES AND AMERICANS.*"

Black spokesmen had made clear their feelings on their so-called homeland. Africa held little lure for most African Americans, particularly the freedmen and freedwomen. "But if Blacks no longer thought of themselves as Africans," Dorothy Sterling asks, "who were they?"[35]

David Walker wrote: "'Niger' is a word derived from the Latin, which was used by the old Romans to designate inanimate [objects] which were black: such as soot, pot, wood, house, &c. Also, animals which they considered inferior to the human species, as a black horse, cow, hog, &c. The white Americans have applied this term to Africans, by way of reproach for our color, to aggravate and heighten our miseries, because they have their feet on our throats."[36] It is worth emphasizing that Walker's *Appeal* was addressed to "the Coloured Citizens of the World," not to its Negro Citizens.

Garrison took a special interest in this debate, running many letters to the editor in *The Liberator* about it. On June 4, 1831, a woman who signed her name only as "Ella" posited: "Why do our friends as well as our enemies call us 'Negroes'? We feel it to be a term of reproach, and could wish our friends would call us by some other name. If you, Sir, or one of your correspondents would condescend to answer this question, we would esteem it a favor."[37]

Three months later, another person came up with a novel suggestion: "The term 'colored' is not a good one. Whenever used, it recalls to mind the offensive distinctions of color. The name 'African' is more objectionable yet, and is no more correct than 'Englishman' would be to a native-born citizen of the United States. The colored citizen is an American of African descent. Cannot a name be found that will explain these two facts? I suggest one, and I beg our readers to reflect on it before you reject it as unsuitable. It is 'Afric-American' or, written in one word, 'Africamerican.' It asserts that most important truth, that the colored citizen is as truly a citizen of the United States as the white."[38]

But "Afric-American" raised hackles. "A Subscriber and Citizen of the United States" wrote, "The suggestion is as absurd as the sound of the name is inharmonious. It is true that we should have a distinct appellation—we being the only people in America who feel all the accumulated injury which pride and prejudice can suggest. But sir, since we have been so long distinguished by the title 'men of color,' why make this change, so uncouth and jargon-like? A change we do want and a change we will have. When it comes, we shall be called citizens of the *United States and Americans*."[39]

But some people advocated using the term "colored." James McCune Smith, as we saw, still preferred it as late as 1859. In fact, two men, the aforementioned Reverend Samuel E. Cornish and New York City journalist Philip A. Bell, founded a magazine in 1837 called *The Colored American*. In their first issue, they explained the logic behind their choice of "colored" in the title of the periodical:

> The editor, aware of the diversity of opinion in reference to the title of this "Paper" thinks it not amiss to state some reasons for selecting this name.

> Many would gladly rob us of the endeared name "AMERICAN," a distinction more emphatically belonging to us than five-sixths of this nation and one that we will never yield.
>
> But why colored? Because our circumstances require special action. We have in view objects peculiar to ourselves and in contradistinction from the mass. How, then, shall we be known and our interests presented but by some distinct, specific name—and what appellation is so inoffensive, so acceptable, as COLORED PEOPLE—COLORED AMERICANS?[40]

Still, not everybody liked the word "colored." William Whipper, the Black businessman and abolitionist from Pennsylvania, put forth a motion at the Fifth Annual Convention for the Improvement of the Free People of Color in the United States in 1835: "That we recommend as far as possible to our people to abandon the use of the word 'colored' when either speaking or writing concerning themselves; and especially to remove the title of African from their institutions, the marbles of churches, &c."

The resolution was adopted unanimously "after an animated and interesting discussion." In 1835 the Colored Convention members inaugurated a new organization that fully reflected its turn to moral suasion: the American Moral Reform Society. While state conventions would continue, 1835 marked the final national convention for eight years. The AMRS now represented the Colored Convention movement at the national level.[41]

The 1835 Declaration of Sentiments promoted as its "rallying points" education, temperance, the economy, and "Universal Liberty." But the most dramatic and controversial event of the convention, and the topic for which the AMRS would become known, came from its rejection of racial language altogether. Whipper's proposals "to abandon the use of the word 'colored' . . . and especially to remove the title of African from their institutions" were embraced.

"Whipper was not merely a seasoned delegate," the historian Joan L. Bryant explains. "He was a pivotal figure in the national conventions." The only man who had attended each national convention, he had played the key role in shifting their focus away from emigration. Now he called for moral reform beyond "complexional differences." Debates over naming the race mattered less than eliminating naming altogether. Few convention delegates would have contested the point on an intellectual level. But how would Black reformers reach any practical goal without the explicit acknowledgment of racial discrimination? The AMRS never answered that question.[42]

After all, even the AMRS could not abandon racial terminology altogether. The 1836 convention stressed helping the "colored population," and Black people responded, at least at first. In 1837, "moral reformers counted 100 people among its initial members and delegates," Bryant writes. "Forty individuals from this group—a number comparable to the size of the 1830 convention—officially participated in the proceedings."

The 1837 national convention was a turning point. Whipper appealed to Christianity. Racism was wrong, and the "general assertion that superiority of mind is the natural offspring of a fair complexion, arrays itself against the experience of the past and present age, and both natural and physiological science." Glaude cites the last phrase as evidence that Whipper used moral reform and religion to counter the rising tide of "race science," which purported to prove that race was an essential, immutable, biological characteristic that indicated a person's superiority if white and inferiority if Black.

Universal benevolence tolerated no racial distinctions. At the same time, reformers recognized but could do nothing about white clergymen who connected slavery to the Christianity that Whipper and his allies supported. Religious enslavers did not reckon with the logic of universal human rights. They ignored it, or, perhaps more accurately, subsumed it into the system of slavery.[43]

The 1837 meeting ended with President James Forten, the friend of the late Paul Cuffee, officially banning references to race. The discussion did not end there.

Cornish, the editor of *The Colored American*, attended the convention and came away disturbed: "We found a Purvis, a Whipper, and others, (of whose Christian benevolence and cultivated intellect we have so many and such strong evidences), vague, wild, indefinite and confused in their views. They created shadows, fought the wind, and bayed at the moon for more than three days."[44]

The debate was not about integration versus separatism. Whipper did not deny the importance of African heritage. He invited the participation of white people but still criticized the overarching white power structure. His was a question of language and its meaning. As Americans debated what certain groups want or ought to be called, just as they do now, Whipper opted out. Racial terminology, in his view, validated racial hierarchies and white supremacy.

Many African Americans, like Cornish, castigated this idea, even as they had to agree with the larger point. Cornish admitted he was "as much opposed to complexional distinctions as brother Whipper or any other man." Cornish's central point exposed what Whipper's opponents viewed as the fatal flaw of his reasoning: If their discrimination was based on their race, how could they address it without discussing their race? Black people certainly did not believe that distinctions of color reflected essentialist racial differences. White use of distinctions did, however, discriminate against African Americans. The malleability of the term "colored" also affected the debate. It meant different things to different users. As Bryant puts it, "It was variously a phenotypic description, a designation of social circumstances, and a caste label. The indefinite character of the term meant that people attached multiple and conflicting meanings to it simultaneously."[45]

Ignoring words would not alter the forces they represented. "Words are used as the signs of our ideas, and whenever they perform this office, or are truly significant of the ideas for which they stand, they accomplish the object of their invention," wrote William Watkins of Baltimore, a cofounder with Grice of the Legal Rights Association, in a letter to the 1838 AMRS convention. The letter was not read at the convention but was instead published in *The Colored American*. Watkins wrote of the word "colored": "Custom has fixed its meaning in reference to a particular people in this country, and from this decision, however arbitrary, there is, I am sure, no successful appeal. Again, to decry the use of the word, colored, on account of some questionable inaccuracy in its applicability to us, is an argument, which if successful, would blot out from our English vocabularies certain words of established usage."[46]

In 1841 Whipper criticized a state convention at Albany, New York, for its focus on racial differences. An unknown writer named Sidney responded with letters to *The Colored American*. Racial terminology, in his view, did not have to be destructive. "Whenever a people are oppressed, peculiarly (not complexionally), distinctive organization or action, is required on the part of the oppressed, to destroy that oppression. The colored people of this country are oppressed; therefore the colored people are required to act in accordance with this fundamental principle." Ignoring race would never be effective. "We are afflicted with colorphobia," Sidney wrote, "and it is going to work wonders with us—wonders like those Moses wrought in Egypt—of fearful nature, and destructive tendency; unless the right means are used to effect a radical cure."[47]

He continued:

> We do not think that by watering and preserving the plant that perfumes our room that *therefore* we dislike all other plants in the world. We do not believe that in loving our own mother's sons, our brothers, that therefore we exclude mankind. In fine we have no sympathy with the cosmopoliting [*sic*] disposition which tramples upon all nationality.
>
> And pray, for what are we to turn around and bay the whole human family? Why are we to act different from all others in this important matter? Why, because we *happen* to be—COLORED.

That we are colored is a fact, an undeniable fact. That we are descendants of Africans is true. We affirm there is nothing in it that we need to be ashamed of, yea, rather much that we may be proud of.

For ourselves we are quite well satisfied. And we intend, in all our public efforts, to go to the power-holding body and tell them, "Colored as we are, *black* though we may be, yet we demand our rights, the same rights other citizens have."[48]

A final word on this subject was spoken by the great Henry Highland Garnet. One of the first advocates of militant abolitionism, Garnet was a fascinating figure who would become a foe of Frederick Douglass, who thought Garnet's ideas too radical to be practical. In fact, their debates about militancy, armed struggle, and revolution were among the most heated in the antebellum Black community.

Like Douglass, Garnet was born enslaved in Maryland, but in 1824, when he was nine years old, his family escaped to Pennsylvania. They had been given permission to attend a funeral and ran away instead. He was very well educated, attending the African Free School and the Phoenix High School in New York City. From there, he attended the Noyes Academy in Canaan, New Hampshire, and went on to graduate in 1839 from the Oneida

Theological Institute. In 1840, his leg was amputated following an injury he incurred while playing sports. After 1842, he served as a Presbyterian minister, pastoring in a variety of churches.[49]

He delivered his most famous speech in 1843, at the annual National Negro Convention in Buffalo. His "Call to Rebellion" alienated him from Douglass and from his mentor, William Lloyd Garrison. The speech was so controversial that it did not appear in the convention minutes. It spread by word of mouth and then received wider readership when he published a "slightly modified" version in 1848 alongside a reprint of David Walker's *Appeal*, an appropriate choice.

Garnet's central point was that enslaved people had a responsibility as Christians to resist slavery by any means necessary, including violence: "The forlorn condition in which you are placed, does not destroy your moral obligation to God. You are not certain of heaven, because you suffer yourselves to remain in a state of slavery, where you cannot obey the commandments of the Sovereign of the universe. . . . THEREFORE IT IS YOUR SOLEMN AND IMPERATIVE DUTY TO USE EVERY MEANS, BOTH MORAL, INTELLECTUAL, AND PHYSICAL THAT PROMISES SUCCESS."

God would reward the people who resisted slavery,

Garnet argued. Resistance meant potential violence, violence that an enslaved person should, indeed *must*, embrace. If not the enslaved themselves, then who?

He concluded his fiery speech with a call to arms: "Let your motto be resistance! resistance! resistance! No oppressed people have ever secured their liberty without resistance. What kind of resistance you had better make, you must decide by the circumstances that surround you, and according to the suggestion of expediency. Brethren, adieu! Trust in the living God. Labor for the peace of the human race, and remember that you are four millions."

The crowd "was literally infused with tears." After multiple votes the convention rejected officially adopting Garnet's address. Among the nays was Frederick Douglass, who thought Garnet's call for violence was misguided, irresponsible, and doomed to fail. He encouraged opponents of slavery to try "moral means a little longer." He carried the day, although it would be only a few years until he came around to Garnet's way of thinking.[50]

After the Fugitive Slave Act of 1850 brought slavery to the doorsteps of all free Black people in the North, emigration again became a dominant topic of discussion, at the conventions and beyond. Garnet and Martin Delany became the most prominent supporters of emigration; Delany even called a national emigration convention, which occurred in Cleveland from August 24 to 26, 1854.

In 1849 Garnet helped to found the African Civilization Society. He was now an advocate of the emigration of Black people to Mexico, Liberia, or the West Indies, where he had traveled as a cabin boy on ships bound for Cuba. He called for a colony to be founded in Yorubaland, in western Nigeria, and for separate sections of the United States to be founded as Black colonies.[51]

Garnet abandoned his emigrationist efforts when the Civil War broke out, and he worked to have Lincoln allow Black men to fight. The final national convention before the end of the Civil War was held in Syracuse, from October 4 to 7, 1864. The Emancipation Proclamation of 1863 and the valor of Black troops led convention delegates to focus less on emigration and more on the political possibilities for African Americans in the United States. More than 140 African American delegates attended, including Douglass and Garnet, who helped found the National Equal Rights League.

On February 12, 1865, Garnet became the first Black minister to deliver a sermon in the House of Representatives. Garnet's last wish was to live and die in Liberia. He got his wish: in 1881 he was named minister to Liberia. Sadly, he died just two months after his arrival to take up his post. He was given a state funeral by the Liberian government and was buried at Palm Grove Cemetery in Monrovia. Even Frederick Douglass mourned his loss.

His portrait hangs in the Hall of Capitols, in the Cox Corridors of the Capitol building, as part of a mural painted in 1973–74 called *Civil Rights Bill Passes, 1866*.

Garnet left us a last word about the politics and value of the debate over naming that Dorothy Sterling dubbed the "namestakes": "How unprofitable it is for us to spend our golden moments in long and solemn debate upon the question whether we shall be called 'Africans,' 'Colored Americans' or 'Africo Americans' or 'Blacks.' The question should be, my friends, shall we arise and act like men, and cast off this terrible yoke?"[52]

◇

CHAPTER THREE

Who's Your Daddy?

FREDERICK DOUGLASS AND THE
POLITICS OF SELF-REPRESENTATION

Almost as soon as Phillis Wheatley's book of poems hit the shelves of booksellers in London in 1773, other formerly enslaved Africans, in England and America, began to publish a different sort of book: autobiographical narrative accounts of the authors' time spent in slavery. They always told the story of how they learned to read and write, and always, always, of course, of their escape to freedom.

These narratives constituted a new genre of literature; today we call them the slave narratives. They combine autobiography with carefully crafted, cogent attacks on the institution of human bondage. The slave narratives were enormously popular. In the eighteenth century, the 1789 narrative of Olaudah Equiano reached enviable heights of renown. But the most popular of all these slave narratives was to come some five decades later, in 1845, the runaway bestseller by a twenty-seven-year-old fugitive slave whose name at birth was Frederick Augustus Washington Bailey.

In Baltimore, Bailey changed his name to Frederick Stanley; in New York, to Frederick Johnson. Finally, upon reaching New Bedford, Massachusetts, where he worked in the shipping industry, he adopted the name by which he became one of the best known of all figures of the nineteenth century: Frederick Douglass. He took his new surname from a literary character, the Black Douglas, in Sir Walter Scott's poem of 1810, *The Lady of the Lake*, adding the second *s* himself,[1] while opting to keep his first given name, Frederick. "I must hold on to that, to preserve a sense of my identity," he wrote in his first memoir.[2]

Unlike most other enslaved people, Douglass could trace his Black ancestry back several generations. Douglass's mother was enslaved by the Bailey family, which had deep roots in slavery in Maryland. Even if he had wanted to keep the name Bailey—although one assumes he was eager to shed the name of his white enslaver, who was almost certainly his father—he had little choice, initially at least: he was a fugitive, a commodity on the lam. Enslaved Black men and women in flight to the North could be returned to their enslaver's possession if they were apprehended, especially after the notorious Fugitive Slave Act of 1850. While the law didn't recognize a surname that an enslaved person used to describe themselves, enforcers certainly used that surname to their benefit when hunting down runaways.

Enslaved people recognized the importance of naming. Naming oneself, protecting that name from generation to generation, and quite possibly protecting oneself from slave catchers, was an assertion of one's humanity and individuality. Knowing the identities and names of one's ancestors, especially one's father and mother, was of great importance, too—and considering the abomination of family separation, not something to be taken for granted. In his 1901 autobiography, *Up from Slavery*, Booker T. Washington noted that there were two things "practically all" formerly enslaved people did after Emancipation: change their name in some way, even if it meant just adding a middle initial, which they called their "entitles"; and walk off the plantation on which they had been held in bondage, even if the only thing they did was to turn around and walk back.[3]

The publication of books written by people who had escaped slavery was, first and last, political, and slave narratives were critical to the antislavery movement. What more powerful tool or weapon could be used to fight slavery and the slave trade than the written testimony of those who had been enslaved themselves, men and women who, by performing the act of writing, could simultaneously attest to the evils of enslavement *and* refute the claims that the African lacked reason or couldn't write poetry? Their writings were proof that the Black person was neither beast nor animal nor first cousin of the apes. After 1831, the year in which William Lloyd Garrison began to publish his antislavery newspaper *The Liberator*, followed a year later by the formation of the New England Anti-Slavery Society, the American antislavery movement would encourage the most articulate of the fugitives to write about their experiences under slavery from their own point of view.

The movement even subsidized the publication of these books, including, eventually, the bestseller that Frederick Douglass would publish in 1845. Would-be authors were guided in their narratives from start to finish. They talked their books out loud on the lecture circuit, and after practice and repetitions, they wrote their stories down. The abolitionist lecture circuit was, in effect, a school for creative writing.

The trope of the talking book, as we have seen, was a powerful device in the slave narratives published around the turn of the nineteenth century. It built on a tradition that incorporated riffing revisions—covers, essentially—between 1772 and 1811. The formerly enslaved man John Jea actually literalized this metaphor in his 1811 slave narrative by claiming that, after he had fasted for days and days and beseeched God to teach him to read and write, an angel appeared in his room in the middle of the night and taught him to do just that, not only in English but also in Dutch, on the spot. After Jea turned the trope of the talking book inside out, there was little opportunity for other writers to use the technique in any noteworthy or innovative way.[4] But it would find a new form in the second generation of slave narratives, published after 1830.

Some three decades after John Jea, Frederick Douglass would make the text speak in another way; for Douglass, learning to read and write was the pathway to freedom, and literacy was what separated a human being from a beast, a man from an animal, a free man from an enslaved one. He would use this relation between freedom and literacy as a structuring principle of his narrative strategy in the same way that a previous generation of Black writers had used the image of the talking book:

> Very soon after I went to live with Mr. and Mrs. Auld, she very kindly commenced to teach me the A, B, C. After I had learned this, she assisted me in learning to spell words of three or four letters. Just at this point of my progress, Mr. Auld

found out what was going on, and at once forbade Mrs. Auld to instruct me further, telling her, among other things, that it was unlawful, as well as unsafe, to teach a slave to read. To use his own words, further, he said, "If you give a nigger an inch, he will take an ell [which is about eighteen inches]. A nigger should know nothing but to obey his master—to do as he is told to do. Learning would *spoil* the best nigger in the world. Now," said he, "if you teach that nigger (speaking of myself) how to read, there would be no keeping him. It would forever unfit him to be a slave. He would at once become unmanageable, and of no value to his master. As to himself, it could do him no good, but a great deal of harm. It would make him discontented and unhappy." These words sank deep into my heart, stirred up sentiments within that lay slumbering, and called into existence an entirely new train of thought. It was a new and special revelation, explaining dark and mysterious things, with which my youthful understanding had struggled, but struggled in vain. I now understood what had been to me a most perplexing difficulty—to wit, the white man's power to enslave the black man. It was a grand achievement, and I prized it highly. From that moment, I understood the pathway from slavery to freedom.[5]

Once he learned to read, Douglass said, running away to freedom was inevitable. Even here, Douglass was responding to the Enlightenment debate about the nature of the African, about his or her capacity to possess and express reason. The novelist Ishmael Reed summed it up this way: the slave who learned to read and write was the first slave to run away.[6] Judging from the slave narratives, this was often true.

But escaping slavery was certainly not as widespread as once believed, nor as the myths of the size of the Underground Railroad would suggest. Very few people escaped their enslavement; after all, if hundreds of thousands of enslaved men, women, and children had escaped through the Underground Railroad, slavery would have collapsed long before the Civil War.

Maybe as many as twenty-five thousand achieved this incredible feat. Of the enslaved persons who made it across the Mason-Dixon Line to freedom, 102 published book-length slave narratives. This is the largest body of literature ever created in the history of the world by persons who had been enslaved. By contrast, there is only one slave narrative published by a formerly enslaved person in Cuba in the nineteenth century, and Cuba received almost one million Africans directly from the African continent, two and a half times more than the United States did.

Most scholars would agree that Frederick Douglass was the most eloquent among all of these authors. He escaped bondage in 1838 and became a part of the antislavery lecture circuit, starting on Nantucket in 1841. The abolitionists had him rehearse his story before live audiences for four years. His speeches were covered by newspaper reporters, who transcribed them using shorthand. His words were therefore widely read and could be scrutinized, in the North and in the South, even by his former enslaver back home in Maryland, to ascertain their veracity.

Veracity and verification were critical to the abolitionists' project. They had been burned less than a decade before Douglass published his narrative. The publication of *The Narrative of James Williams, an American Slave, who was for Several Years a Driver on a Cotton Plantation in Alabama*, published in 1838 by the American Anti-Slavery Society, made the abolitionists realize the importance of, as the saying goes, truth in advertising.

On New Year's Day, 1838, James Williams made his way to the Anti-Slavery Society's offices in New York, where he told a captivating story. He explained that he was born enslaved in Powhatan County, Virginia, in 1805, and that he had been well treated in Virginia by his owner, George Larrimore. Eventually, Williams would marry an enslaved woman named Harriet who lived on a different plantation, in the possession of a different enslaver. A white minister presided over the ceremony. They had four children, two of whom died in infancy.

Upon George Larrimore's death, James Williams's

new owner, George Larrimore, Jr., moved 214 enslaved Black people from Virginia to Alabama, to a plantation owned by his wife in Greene County. Williams would be separated, temporarily he was told, from Harriet and their two children, the youngest of whom was two months old. Mother and babies were left behind. Though Williams's enslaver promised to return him to Virginia, he broke his word, leaving Williams at the whim of an evil overseer named Huckstep. Huckstep made Williams a driver— essentially a Black overseer, the enslaved person forced to manage and punish his enslaved brethren. Williams detailed the violent atrocities he was forced to carry out at Huckstep's command, among them whipping a pregnant woman and sending bloodhounds after runaways. He witnessed enslaved people being shot as well as one man being made to eat his own Bible as punishment for practicing Christianity.

At one point, Williams refused to whip a woman under Huckstep's orders, whipping the tree she was tied to instead to make it look like he had done the job. But when Williams was ratted out to Huckstep, the overseer gave *him* 250 lashes.[7]

Williams eventually ran away, finding shelter with the Creek Indians. He hid in the woods and waded through creeks for months, following the North Star. At long last, in December 1837, he crossed the Mason-Dixon Line and made it to freedom in Carlisle, Pennsylvania. He quickly relocated to New York City, walking into the Anti-Slavery Society's office on January 1 and telling his story.

The white abolitionists embraced Williams. In him, they had found an enslaved man who was articulate and presentable. They wasted no time in publishing his story: his was the ultimate critique of the evils of slavery. He told his story to none other than the great Quaker poet and abolitionist John Greenleaf Whittier, with at least the implicit understanding that he would receive safe passage to England in exchange. They worked night and day and completed the book in three weeks, on January 24, 1838. Three weeks later, on February 15, the book was in print, with a preface by Whittier. Because Williams was illiterate, Whittier actually penned the entire narrative. It was an unmitigated success; within six months, it had gone through three printings. In November, Williams sailed for Liverpool, England.

He was never heard from again.[8]

The basis for the book—that Williams had escaped slavery—was true. The same could not be said for the details that formed his *Narrative*. According to the scholar Hank Trent, a man named J. B. Rittenhouse, the editor of a newspaper called *The Alabama Beacon*, reviewed the book and found that not one of the white people named in the book ever lived in Alabama. He also discovered that the dates and distances in the book were incorrect. Most damning of all, he claimed that Huckstep, the evil overseer, never existed. Following an investigation, James Birney and Lewis Tappan of the American Anti-Slavery Society conceded in *The Emancipator*, on October 25, 1838, that they were suspending sales of the book because they "cannot with propriety ask for the confidence of the community in any of the statements contained in the narrative."[9]

The publication of the falsified narrative was a grave embarrassment to the abolitionists. After all, they had advertised Williams's book around the idea that, at last, "THE SLAVE HAS SPOKEN FOR HIMSELF." They had been looking for an enslaved American as articulate as Equiano had been in the previous century in London, and in Williams they thought they had found him. The search began anew for another spokesman, someone equally articulate, to take Williams's place. The movement soon found its man in Frederick Douglass.[10]

Frederick Douglass was an abolitionist's dream: a tall, handsome mulatto who could read and write. He also was a natural orator. Douglass had been enslaved in Talbot County, Maryland. Eventually, after learning to read and write, he defeated his evil overseer, Mr. Gore, in an epic battle. It was then that Douglass realized the road to freedom was paved with literacy. After marrying a free Negro in Baltimore, he escaped, disguised as a sailor, carrying free papers that he himself had forged. He took the train from Baltimore to Philadelphia, where he was now free. After moving to New York with his wife, they relocated to New Bedford, Massachusetts. In August 1841, he attended an antislavery rally on Nantucket, and there, quite spontaneously, "he rose and found his voice." William Lloyd Garrison had been speaking; after Douglass spoke, the abolitionists hired him on the spot to be a lecturer on the antislavery circuit. To vouch for the veracity of his tale, they made him recite it on the lecture circuit for four years before he could publish it, so that, if he was not telling the truth, his lies would be exposed. In 1845, he published his *Narrative*.

Frederick Douglass became the undisputed, unequaled superstar on the antislavery circuit because he could write and speak so well. People would come from miles around to hear him hold forth for hours about the evils of slavery. From his book sales and speaking engagements, he became quite wealthy. In the 1855 introduction to *My Bondage and My Freedom*, James McCune Smith, echoing Emerson's definition of the "Representative Man," published five years earlier, called him "a Representative American man—a type of his countrymen."[11] He was a friend of Abraham Lincoln's; he edited his own newspapers; he traveled widely in Europe and even went to Egypt with his second wife, a wealthy white woman named Helen Pitts. He had several presidential appointments, including serving as the consul-general to Haiti between 1889 and 1891. Having sat for more than 160 portraits over the course of his lifetime, cultivating his image to maximize his dignity and accomplishments, Douglass was the most photographed American in the entire nineteenth century.[12]

But one thing always haunted Frederick Douglass.

On March 16, 1894, Douglass, by then in his late seventies, took a train from his home in Anacostia, a neighborhood of Washington, DC, north to Baltimore, where he visited Dr. Thomas Sears, the grandson of his former enslavers, Thomas and Lucretia Auld. Though he had already written three autobiographies, Douglass was still searching for one elusive fact of his birth. Peter Walker observes in his 1978 book *Moral Choices* that Douglass was forever looking for the "lost past" that slavery had taken from him, even as he re-created (and revised) it in his autobiographies. Incredibly, Douglass got on the train that day and went to Baltimore for one reason: to discover his actual birthday. He did not want to die without knowing the exact day that he was born. As Walker notes, "The childhood unhappiness of having no birthday was never overcome. To the end of his life the mystery of his birth-day was [in Douglass's words] 'a serious trouble.'"[13]

After the meeting, Douglass wrote down in his diary what he considered the crucial genealogical facts gleaned from Sears:

> Capt. Thomas Auld was born 1795
>
> Amanda Auld, his daughter was born Jan 28 1826
>
> Thomas, son of Hugh and Sophia Auld was born Jan: 1824
>
> Capt Aaron Anthony [Douglass's first owner, the father of Lucretia Auld], Died Nov 14 1823

From these facts, Douglass concluded that "the death of Aaron Anthony makes me fix the year in which I was sent to live with Mr. Hugh Auld in Baltimore, as 1825."[14] As Peter Walker was the first to show, Douglass hinged his whole effort to solve the mystery of the day of his birth on this single date, the most solid date he could find, using it to reason backward. This was the last entry that Frederick Douglass ever made in his diary. Douglass boarded that train back to Washington and reflected ruefully that he had still no evidence of his exact birthday.

Less than a year later, Douglass died at his home in Anacostia, at his calculated age of seventy-eight. Even his obituary in *The New York Times* noted, "The exact date of his birth is unknown."[15]

Prior to knowing the story of Frederick Douglass, what might be considered one of the single defining characteristics that distinguished an enslaved Black person from a free white person? The list is long: Someone who could be beaten at any time for any reason. Someone who could be raped at will. Someone who had no property rights and, indeed, was property herself or himself. All of these horrors were true. But who is defined as a "slave," according to someone made to live as a slave? In other words, what absence or lack or deprivation did Douglass mention in the first paragraph of his slave narrative?

> I was born in Tuckahoe, near Hillsborough, and about twelve miles from Easton, in Talbot county, Maryland. I have no accurate knowledge of my age, never having seen any authentic record containing it. By far the larger part of the slaves know as little of their ages as horses know of theirs, and it is the wish of most masters within my knowledge to keep their slaves thus ignorant. I do not remember to have ever met a slave who could tell of his birthday. They seldom come nearer to it than planting-time, harvest-time, cherry-time, spring-time, or fall-time. A want of information concerning my own was a source of unhappiness to me even during childhood. The white children

could tell their ages. I could not tell why I ought to be deprived of the same privilege. I was not allowed to make any inquiries of my master concerning it. He deemed all such inquiries on the part of a slave improper and impertinent, and evidence of a restless spirit. The nearest estimate I can give makes me now between twenty-seven and twenty-eight years of age. I come to this, from hearing my master say, some time during 1835, I was about seventeen years old.[16]

Douglass charted the differences between slavery and freedom through a series of what we call binary oppositions, and this is one of them. Not knowing his birth date marked the unbridgeable difference between being a slave and being free. Specifically, white boys and girls could know their birthdays; enslaved Black boys and girls could not. Many other binary oppositions appear in the first chapter: Douglass's mother is Black; his father is white. He sees his mother only four or five times, and only at night; he sees his father only in the day. His mother comes to him from a nearby plantation on foot; his white father rides on a carriage drawn by horses. His mother is a metaphor for nature, his father for culture. His mother is enslaved; his father is his enslaver. He tells the reader this three times by the fifth paragraph. Douglass calls this "the double relation of master and father."

These binary oppositions continue until he reverses

them, turning them upside down. He does so through a chiasmus, a rhetorical device whose name comes from the Greek work for "X-shaped." In a chiasmus, the first and second part of a sentence are essentially written in reverse order. The most famous chiasmus in American history is John F. Kennedy's "Ask not what your country can do for you; ask what you can do for your country." Douglass's signature chiasmus appears at the structural center of his brilliantly crafted narrative: "You have seen how a man was made a slave; you shall see how a slave was made a man."[17]

Douglass turns the world that the planters made upside down, showing that it is they who are the real savages, the real beasts, the real animals, because they are the real or literal cannibals. Why? Because they trade in human flesh; in other words, metaphorically, they consume their own children whom they have fathered through the women and girls they hold in bondage, committing rape and adultery, keeping them as property and then selling them, violating a sacred tenet of Western civilization: that a child will follow the condition of their father, and not their *mother*. Had these enslaved mulattos been allowed to follow the condition of their fathers, they would have been free at birth. They were not allowed to do so because they were still considered property, even though they were half white. And mulattos were very valuable property. Even mixed children, because of the economics of slavery, unlike every other child in America, followed the condition of their mothers.

Douglass wrote two bestselling slave narratives, one in 1845 and the other in 1855. He also published a full-length autobiography in 1881, long after he had become a world-famous statesman. Even though perhaps no one's words were more closely scrutinized than those of Frederick Douglass, he somehow avoided being questioned about a most remarkable series of revisions of crucial facts about his enslavement. In fact, we might consider these the most crucial facts of all in the life of any human being. In an astonishing act of literary legerdemain, Douglass managed to change dramatically his accounts of his relationship to and his descriptions of both his mother and his father, even completely transforming his accounts of their identities.

In 1845, Douglass penned the famous line "My father was my master; my master was my father," mentioning the connection between master and father four times in the first seven paragraphs of the book. In the third paragraph, he writes: "My father was a white man. The opinion was also whispered that my master was my father; but of the correctness of this opinion, I know nothing; the means of knowing was withheld from me." Two paragraphs later, he continues: "Called thus suddenly away, [my mother] left me without the slightest intimation of who my father was. The whisper that my master was my father, may or may not be true; and, true or false, it is of but little consequence to my purpose whilst the fact remains, in all its glaring odiousness, that slaveholders have ordained, and by law established, that the children of slave women shall in all cases follow the condition of their mothers; and this is done too obviously to administer to their own lusts, and make a gratification of their wicked desires profitable as well as pleasurable; for by this cunning arrangement, the slaveholder, in cases not a few, sustains to his slaves the double relation of master and father." Another two paragraphs on, he says: "it is certain that slavery at the south must soon become unscriptural; for thousands are ushered into the world, annually, who, like myself, owe their existence to white fathers, and those fathers most frequently their own masters."[18] By 1855, he addresses his father's complexion with hesitant certainty. "My father was a white man, or nearly white."[19] But in the final version, in 1881, Frederick Douglass states plainly: "of my father I know nothing."[20]

His mother stood on the other side of the binary. In 1845, Douglass shared that he saw her only four or five times, and only at night. He "received the tidings of her death with much the same emotions I should have probably felt at the death of a stranger." A decade later, the image he projects of his mother is more crisply drawn. She becomes tall, splendidly proportioned, glossy-dark, regular featured. In one memorable incident, his mother appears suddenly to give him food and to protect him from cruel Aunt Katy, who had not allowed him to eat that day. Here, Douglass learns that night that he is "somebody's child." She sweeps her son into her "strong, protecting arms."[21] In that narrative, he also writes of his mother's surprising literacy: "I learned, after my mother's death, that she could read, and that she was the only one of all of the slaves and colored people in Tuckahoe who enjoyed that advantage. How she acquired this knowledge, I know not, for Tuckahoe is the last place in the world where she would be apt to find facilities for learning. I can, therefore, fondly and proudly ascribe to her an earnest love of knowledge."[22] In 1881, the final narrative, Douglass credits his mother further. Peter Walker writes that, for Douglass, "It was she alone who enabled him to become a writer and speaker; she gave Douglass his voice. . . . [Douglass] was driving himself deeper and deeper into a proud identification with Harriet Bailey who above all else was a Black slave."[23] He had even found a picture in a book that reminded him of his departed mother, in James Prichard's *Natural History of Man*. In this vision, though, his "mother" was not a woman at all, but a man, and not a Black African, but an

Egyptian—the pharaoh Ramses II. And that appears in his second slave narrative, published in 1855, and then again in his autobiography of 1881.

Over the course of his three autobiographies, Douglass reduced his father from a white man who was his master to an invisible man, while simultaneously transforming his mother from someone he saw only four or five times and only at night into the pharaoh Ramses II or into the most eloquent, literate Black woman, and indeed, enslaved person—male or female—in all of Talbot County, Maryland.

Only Frederick Douglass knew the answer to the question of which of these descriptions about his mother and father was true, and he took that secret with him to his grave. Does that mean that Frederick Douglass, the *replacement* for James Williams, in effect, "pulled a James Williams" on the abolitionists right under their noses, and they didn't even notice? Is the value in reading Douglass's slave narrative diminished because of these contradictions?

We can begin to understand why Douglass did this from his own writings. In 1854, in "The Claims of the Negro, Ethnologically Considered," written a year before he published his second slave narrative, *My Bondage and My Freedom*, Frederick Douglass wrote: "intellect is uniformly derived from the *maternal* side. Mulattoes, in this country, may almost wholly boast of Anglo-Saxon *male* ancestry."[24]

There was absolutely no scientific evidence to support Douglass's provocative claim, but he made it anyway.[25] When white abolitionists tried to hold Douglass up as an example of Black intellect and the equality of the so-called races, the equality of the African with the European, white critics were convinced that he derived all his intelligence from his white father; that his white father's genes were expressing themselves *in spite of* his African genetic heritage. They had no scientific evidence to support their claim, either. Douglass went through these gyrations to refute the charges that his deep intellect came from his white father so that he could be utilized, prima facie, as evidence in the battle for the place of the African on the great chain of being.

◇

CHAPTER FOUR

Who's Your Mama?

THE POLITICS OF DISRESPECTABILITY

In 1994, Evelyn Brooks Higginbotham published *Righteous Discontent*, a brilliant book about the rise of "the politics of respectability" within the African American Black feminist community particularly. The politics of respectability was an ideology of collective racial self-defense adopted to fight back against the rise of white supremacy and the institutionalization of Jim Crow, which the Harvard-trained historian Rayford W. Logan named "the nadir" in race relations in America. This was the absolute low point, the worst time—the forty years or so following the cruel dismantling of Reconstruction in 1877 through the presidency of Woodrow Wilson (1913–1921), one of the most racist presidents ever to occupy the White

House. The nadir ends with the commencement of the New Negro Renaissance (renamed the Harlem Renaissance long after it was over by Langston Hughes, the name that scholars use for this period today), which unfolded coterminously during the Jazz Age of the 1920s.[1]

The nadir saw Jim Crow or de jure segregation become the law of the land, with severe restrictions instated on all aspects of Black life, starting with the passing of the Separate Car Act in Louisiana in 1890, which would lead to racial segregation of public accommodations. That same year the Mississippi Constitutional Convention disenfranchised Black voters, providing a blueprint for the other former Confederate states to follow. By 1900, the gains that had been achieved for African Americans under the Thirteenth, Fourteenth, and Fifteenth Amendments and various Reconstruction acts had largely disappeared. Not only had the Supreme Court in 1896 codified "separate but equal" in *Plessy v. Ferguson*, but the right to vote had become a distant memory for a large percentage of southern Black men, many of whom had been enslaved. Black voters could have had an enormous impact on election outcomes, with 89.7 percent of all African Americans living in the South in 1900.[2] But by this time, for instance, Louisiana had some 1,342 registered Black voters, down from a high of 130,000; and Alabama had 3,000, down from 181,000.[3] Of course, economic suppression, linked to the dismantling of voting rights, was a key part of the establishment of Jim Crow, with the most vivid example seen in the form of neo-slavery called sharecropping. The terror of Jim Crow was real and daily: lynchings were on the increase as part of a terrorist campaign to intimidate Black people from even trying to vote or assume their place as equal citizens.

In response to this onslaught on their rights, Black people attempted to fight back in various ways, perhaps most famously through a strategy articulated in Booker T. Washington's Atlanta Compromise speech, delivered in 1895 at the Cotton States and International Exposition in Atlanta. The most frequently quoted line of that speech affirmed Jim Crow or de jure segregation in social and political matters: "In all things that are purely social we can be as separate as the fingers, yet one as the hand in all things essential to mutual progress."[4] This so-called compromise, Washington hoped, would appease segregationists and enable Black people in the South to achieve economic progress through trade occupations like carpentry, blacksmithing, and making and laying bricks.

Washington advocated for a practical industrial education over what he viewed as the impractical liberal arts: "No race can prosper till it learns that there is as much dignity in tilling a field as in writing a poem," he said. "It is at the bottom of life we must begin, and not at the top."[5]

Writing in his autobiography *Up from Slavery* in 1901, Washington also took aim at W. E. B. Du Bois and Du Bois's hero, Alexander Crummell, when he said, "There was a further feeling that a knowledge, however little of the Greek and Latin languages would make one a very superior human being, something bordering almost on the supernatural."[6]

Frederick Douglass had died in February 1895; in September, with the Atlanta Compromise speech, Washington launched himself into the leadership position of the nation of Negroes. Surprisingly, considering their later undisguised animosity, Du Bois's immediate reaction was one of hearty support. He sent Washington a telegram saying his words were "fitly spoken," and he wrote in *The New York Age* that Washington's ideas "might be the basis of a real settlement between whites and blacks in the South."[7]

Washington's program was the economic response to the rise of Jim Crow, but simultaneously there was a Black cultural response as well. Middle- and upper-middle-class Black people in the North and South fought back symbolically through a complex cultural discourse of their own design. It was a shared ideology expressing itself in a variety of ways, from the women's club movement to sermons in churches and editorials in the Black press. This cultural discourse was designed to show their white class counterparts that a small group of Black people—the group whom Du Bois would name "The Talented Tenth"— embodied the same middle-class Victorian values and morals and aspirations that they did, and that they were different from the African American masses. They dressed like white Victorian middle- and upper-middle-class Americans, and they spoke like them, too, careful to use standard English as opposed to Black dialect. The Black elite would use the production of literature and the visual arts, especially photography, to refute racist stereotypes that were circulating widely in America and Europe about their "nature," crafting an image that stood in stark contrast to the negative images of Black people ever present in cultural forms such as minstrelsy, vaudeville, trade cards (a popular type of advertisement), and postcards. They were, in other words, attempting to show what they were not. Higginbotham aptly named this movement "the politics of respectability."

It was an interracial public discourse, the attempt of well-educated, middle-class Black people to show white Americans—especially white Americans of means, modest or otherwise—that they were "exceptions to the rule," exemplars of the best that the race could achieve. More than that, the members of this group set out to prove that not only were they naturally superior to the mass of Black people, but they were equal to the best that white America had to offer, and they were fully capable of assimilation. They were not inferior by nature or by their essence, and they should be treated accordingly.

The fact that this elite group was "rising," achieving "elevation," making "progress"—three key terms that peppered this discourse—was widely trumpeted in editorials and articles in the Black press and in dozens of biographical dictionaries such as *Progress of a Race; or, The Remarkable Advancement of the American Negro from the Bondage of Slavery, Ignorance and Poverty to the Freedom of Citizenship, Intelligence, Affluence, Honor and Trust*, published in 1902 by John William Gibson and William Henry Crogman. The women and men included in these sorts of compilations suggested what education and cultivation could mean for African Americans.

It was a quasi-religious discourse that stressed conservative moral values and sexual restraint to counter stereotypes of Black people as genetically immoral, licentious, and sexually out of control. A large part of it was aimed at what might be called the valorization of the mother, or the recuperation of the dignity of Black women, who were depicted in the broader popular culture either as light-skinned, hypersexualized Jezebels at one extreme or as dark-skinned, unattractively obese mammies at the other.

These two stereotypes of Black women remain with us today—another binary such as we saw with Frederick

Douglass's multiple versions of his autobiography. It is no accident that the first Black woman to receive an Oscar was Hattie McDaniel for her role as "Mammy" (she had no other name) in *Gone with the Wind*, a Hollywood fantasy of the love that the Black house slaves had for their white masters. Drawing on George Frederickson's term, Higginbotham calls this "romantic racialism."[8]

In other words, the politics of respectability was the flip side of Washington's program, the Black cultural response to the genre of racist imagery I call Sambo art, which was designed to define the race.

A cheap form of chromolithography, a method of making multicolor prints, made it easy to create and widely disseminate tens of thousands of these negative, racist images. Who better to represent the opposite pole to white America visually than Sambo, depicted with the reddest lips and the blackest skin, in every medium possible—postcards, napkins, tea cozies, parlor games like Ten Little Niggers, and a virtual avalanche of color advertisements?

The mammy was crucial to this media campaign. The original Aunt Jemima, Mammy was the safe, grandmotherly type of Black woman, someone who was imagined to love her white enslaver's children more than she loved her own. The image romanticized slavery, stripped it of its brutality toward women (beatings, sexual exploitation, rape), and fabricated nostalgia. This was all happening precisely as white people were sanitizing memories of the Civil War: it was, after all, no longer recalled as "the war to end slavery" but as a war over states' rights.

To counter these images, even the politics of respectability was not enough. Badly wounded by the war against the race, the upper class of the Negro people created a construct called "the New Negro," a carefully crafted image of an ideal Black man and woman who embodied all the virtues of the race and none of the vices.

The phrase "the New Negro" first appeared in print in 1887, in a headline in the *Hartford Daily Courant* that announced "The New Negro in the New South." It was picked up and elaborated upon the following month in the Black newspaper *The Washington Bee*, in an article reading, "We have a new south and a new Negro and the new Negro is coming forth in the platoons of ten thousand deep from the colleges and schools of the Nation, with reverence for the past, but with all his energies bent on the prospect of the future."[9] A journalist employed the phrase in 1895, immediately following his Atlanta speech, to describe Booker T. Washington as the first "New Negro."[10]

We can see, then, in its first iteration, that the trope of the New Negro was almost exclusively associated with the Black upper class, as defined by educational attainments and social status. As one writer put it in the Black newspaper *The Cleveland Gazette* in 1895: "A class of colored people, the 'New Negro,' . . . have arisen Since the War, with education, refinement, and money."[11]

That a "New" Negro existed led to the inevitable conclusion that there was an "Old" Negro that needed to be replaced. The Old Negro, who was the descendant of enslaved men and women, uneducated and unwashed, had become so inextricably intertwined with the racist Sambo images that proliferated in the 1890s decade of Jim Crow that many middle-class Black people decided that his rehabilitation was futile. In answer, they invented a New Negro to represent "the best of the race"—and another binary.

The first full-scale manifestation of the New Negro occurred in 1900, with W. E. B. Du Bois's use of black-and-white photographic portraits in the Exhibit of American Negroes at the historic Paris Exposition (or World's Fair) of 1900. The Exhibit of American Negroes was a brilliant collaboration among Thomas Junius Calloway, Du Bois, Daniel Alexander Payne Murray, and Andrew F. Hilyer. These men themselves epitomized the New Negro—educated, articulate, and successful—and they knew that it "was strategically imperative that Negroes be seen as a proud, productive, and cultured race at Paris," as David Levering Lewis, Du Bois's biographer, puts it, rather than "as a mass of rapists," in Calloway's words. Black people had to present their image as New Negroes to the white world in public, on the unprecedented stage afforded by the Paris Exposition.[12] Du Bois would call it "an honest, straightforward exhibit of a small nation of people, picturing their life and development without apology or gloss, and above all made by themselves."[13]

Du Bois selected 363 photographs—some 150 of Black social, cultural, educational, and economic institutions, and the rest of extremely well-dressed, finely tailored Black individuals—to represent the best of Black achievement since the lifting of the yoke of slavery in 1865. "There are several volumes of photographs of typical Negro faces, which hardly square with conventional American ideas," Du Bois explained.[14] He chose them to represent the variety of skin tones, hair textures, and facial structures (particularly noses, shown in profile), to combat the stereotypical ideas in American popular culture of what Black people looked like. Du Bois designed the Exhibit of American Negroes, as Lewis argues, "to subvert conventional perceptions of the American Negro by presenting to the patronizing curiosity of white spectators a racial universe that was the mirror image of their own uncomprehending, oppressive white world."[15]

The art historian Deborah Willis says that, with their "images of self-empowerment, self-determination, and self-recovery," these photographs themselves constitute a double *mythos*, what Du Bois might have called a "double consciousness": "the one projected on the Black community . . . by its own members" and the one projected on the Black community "by the dominant culture."[16] The Black intelligentsia fought a war against the avalanche of racist, demeaning popular images that sought to dehumanize Black human beings. It's questionable whether this was a war they were winning: while the Talented Tenth could occupy the summit of achievement, prestige, and even wealth within the Black community, they could not achieve meaningful upward social mobility within the larger American society.

Still, it was a war undertaken in earnest for the advantage of the race, as well as for some individuals, who profited handsomely. For instance, Madam C. J. Walker, the first Black female millionaire, attributed to personal hygiene and grooming the success of some of the greatest figures in African American history, including Booker T. Washington and even Frederick Douglass. "Improved appearance responsible," read an ad for her hair care and cosmetics, for the "Amazing Progress of Colored Race."[17]

We might think of this as the Reconstruction of the image of the race, and it was vitally important, even if in retrospect we see a flawed strategy. Unable to change the structures of their oppression, Black leaders embraced individual agency, will, and achievement as the primary ways to fight back against this tidal wave of anti-Black racism. They distributed images of respectable Americans with Black skin in as many magazines and newspapers as they could.

At the same time, within the African American community, another discourse was unfolding underground, the voice of the Black lower classes, the great mass of Black people who most certainly were not New Negroes. We call this "the politics of disrespectability." In contrast to the politics of respectability, the politics of disrespectability was a culturally private discourse; an *intra*racial discourse; a Black-on-Black form of art not intended for white people to hear. (Remember the black box metaphor, the idea that what is on the inside is hidden from and possibly unfathomable to those on the outside.) It embraced folk, vernacular, or lower-class values. It used scandalous language and profanity. It made New Negroes blush. And because it was scandalous, it had to be contained or hidden from the view of the larger American public, if not eliminated from Black cultural practices entirely. The politics of disrespectability was also an antireligious discourse, some would say in league with the devil. Much of it depended on the denigration of the mother, even of her sexualization. These parallel cultural and textual universes are both Black, one unfolding in public in front of white people, the other on the street, in the 'hood, for the consumption of Black people alone. And these two realms of cultural discourse unfolded in parallel universes with their own traditions, unconsciously, side by side, or above-ground and underground. They are the yin and yang of the African American experience—and yet another binary.

These Black vernacular forms seem to have been invented in Harlem and other venues in the urban North during the early years of the Great Migration. The roots of hip-hop are found here in two forms that emerged in the Black community at about the same time as the first New Negro movement, both with their roots in African and African American folklore. First consider the narrative poems that take place in the jungle. They feature three characters: the Monkey, the Lion, and the Elephant. The Lion thinks he is the king of the jungle, but everyone knows that that title belongs to the Elephant. In each poem, the Monkey tricks the Lion into picking a fight with the Elephant, who trounces him every time. The other principal form is called "Shine and the *Titanic*." These stories claim that the sole survivor of the sinking of the *Titanic* was a Black man named Shine who swam all the way from the middle of the Atlantic Ocean back to a bar in Harlem, even before the great ship finally sank.

Even the seemingly prudish Victorians W. E. B. Du Bois and James Weldon Johnson celebrated certain forms of the Black vernacular and made them acceptable, especially in the sacred tradition. Du Bois devotes an entire chapter to Negro spirituals, "Of the Sorrow Songs," in *The Souls of Black Folk*. Johnson wrote of the cakewalk and ragtime in addition to the spirituals. But no respectable figure championed the very risqué forms, such as "Shine" and "The Signifying Monkey," that were most popular with the people. They used Black dialect, and they were vulgar and dirty—and disgustingly misogynistic, when practiced by men. No one was safe, not even "your mama," or, more shockingly, "your grandma, too." "Yo mama" jokes, perhaps surprisingly, are key to understanding the politics of disrespectability. Even the comparatively mild versions of these canonical vernacular forms, quoted below, would have made many of the leading figures of the New Negro Renaissance in the 1920s gasp.

> Down in the jungle about treetop deep
> a signifying Monkey was a wantin' some sleep.
> Now, he'd been tryin' for a week or more,
> and every time he'd go to sleep a damn Lion
> would roar.
> One bright and sunny day
> he told him about a bad bastard over the
> other way.
> Said, "The way he talks, I know it ain't right,

if you two meet there'll be a hell of a fight."
Said, "That wasn't all I heared him say,
why, he done talked about your mama in a hell
    of a way.
He called her a bitch and a dirty whore,
if I hadn't left he'd a called her more.
Why, he [said he] screwed your mother, your
    sister, and your niece,
and the next time he sees your grandma, he's
    gonna ask her for a piece."[18]

Shine, the Black narrator of the *Titanic* toasts, takes aim at the white, rich, and famous, not to mention their mothers, wives, and daughters, as they beg for Shine to save their lives on the sinking ship.

Big man from Wall Street came on the second
    deck.
In his hand he held a book of checks.
He said, "Shine, Shine, if you save poor me,"
say, "I'll make you as rich as any black man
    can be."
Shine said, "You don't like my color and you
    down on my race,
get your ass overboard and give these sharks a
    chase."
Say, the captain's daughter came out on the
    second deck

with her drawers in her hand and brassiere
　　around her neck.
She said, "Shine, Shine, if you save poor me,"
say, "I'll give you all this ass your eyes can see."
Shine said, "There's fish in the ocean, there's
　　whales in the sea,
get your ass overboard and swim like me."[19]

In the collection in which the above poems are included, Bruce Jackson acknowledges that "[n]one of the texts in this book come from women performers. . . . The toasts are often extremely misogynic, so it seems unlikely women would learn or recite them; it would be interesting to know if women have narratives that are equally misandric."[20] Enter the groundbreaking scholar Claudia Mitchell-Kernan, who points out that women engaged in their own versions of the ritual of signifying, turning Black male sexism on its head by reversing the roles.[21] Janie Crawford, the protagonist of Zora Neale Hurston's *Their Eyes Were Watching God*, withstands her husband's insults in public, in his store, until one day she fights back—by talking back, playing her husband's own game and beating him at it. I call this womanist signifying. "Stop mixin' up mah doings wid mah looks, Jody," she says point-blank, standing in the middle of the floor. "Ah'm uh woman every inch of me, and Ah know it. Dat's uh whole lot more'n *you* can say. . . . Talkin' 'bout me lookin' old! When you pull down yo' britches, you look lak de change uh life." One onlooker gasps and says, "Y'all really playin' de dozens tuhnight," and Joe Starks realizes the punishment Janie has meted out is damning and deadly: "she had cast down his empty armor before men and they had laughed, would keep laughing."[22] Laughter, in the case of signifying, is the worst medicine.

Dialect was the linguistic remnant of slavery, the oral sound of Black difference, the sign that the Negroes who used it were unassimilable. Used for racist purposes largely by white performers in blackface on the minstrel stage and in vaudeville routines, dialect was the audible sign of stupidity and the absence of reason, the polar opposite of middle-class values. Many people today continue to make this association. The art forms created by the Black underclass—the people—whether consciously or unconsciously, bear a subversive relationship to the art forms of the New Negro movement, effectively mocking or flat-out rejecting just about everything that the Victorian Black middle and upper-middle class had declared African Americans should aspire to, especially through "The Signifying Monkey" and "Shine and the *Titanic*," but also through the new music called ragtime, the precursor of jazz, a lower-class art form that was not the sort of thing "respectable" Black people would admit to consuming or appreciating. Jean Toomer even complained that the Black middle class was embarrassed by the spirituals, the sacred songs created by enslaved and formerly enslaved women and men. This is what he said:

> There was a valley, the valley of "Cane," with smoke-wreaths during the day and mist at night. A family of back-country Negroes had only recently moved into a shack not too far away. They sang. And this was the first time I'd ever heard the folk-songs and spirituals. They were very rich and sad and joyous and beautiful. But I learned that the Negroes of the town objected to them. They called them "shouting." They had victrolas and player-pianos. So, I realized with deep regret, that the spirituals, meeting ridicule, would be certain to die out. With Negroes also the trend was towards the small town and then the city—and industry and commerce and machines. The folk-spirit was walking in to die on the modern desert. That spirit was so beautiful. Its death was so tragic. Just this seemed the sum of life for me.[23]

In other words, art forms were classed: there was a public middle-class Negro culture and a private southern rural and urban working-class Negro culture. One was created by the upper classes—meant to serve as a public political statement in the battle over the representation of the race—and the other by and for the lower classes, for

consumption by themselves. As far as the more conservative members of the Black middle class were concerned,
all of the Black vernacular cultural forms were of a piece:
Negro folklore, like the spirituals, and later like ragtime
and the blues, like work songs and the oral tradition of
"lying" or tale telling, like the use of Black English or "dialect" in poetry and musical forms, ran counter to the
politics of respectability. So, too, did traditional forms of
African American southern religious rituals, as Toomer
suggests. The sacred as well as the secular could be battle-
grounds over what was "proper," what was "presentable,"
what "hindered the race," and what helped it overcome the
suffocating tide of white supremacy.

The more emotional forms of traditional southern
Black religious worship, like spirit possession ("getting the
Holy Ghost"), doing the Holy Dance in the aisles of the
church, and the ring shout or "shouting," were often subjects of debate among worshippers and their preachers and
bishops. African Methodist Episcopal Bishop Daniel Alexander Payne, for example, who was born free in Charleston, South Carolina, to parents who were members of the
"Brown Elite," first encountered them in the newly freed
South during Reconstruction. To his mind, these were
forms of heathenism and devil worship, all too tangible
retentions of African spiritual practice that arrived with
our ancestors on the slave ships, ways of worshipping and

believing that were "embarrassments to the race," as the commonly used phrase would have it. This is how Payne recounted one such encounter:

> After the sermon they formed a ring, and with coats off sung, clapped their hands and stamped their feet in a most ridiculous and heathenish way. I requested the pastor to go and stop their dancing. At his request they stopped their dancing and clapping of hands, but remained singing and rocking their bodies to and fro. This they did for about fifteen minutes. I then went, and taking their leader by the arm requested him to desist and to sit down and sing in a *rational* manner. I told him also that it was a heathenish way to worship and disgraceful to themselves, the race, and the Christian name.[24]

For Payne, these cultural practices were vestiges both of African "pagan worship" and remnants of slavery, and through admonishment and the threat of excommunication, he did his best to stamp them out.

Remnants of slavery were best left behind in the residue of history back on the plantation, and Africa, whose stereotypical portrayals had understandably been absorbed by many African Americans, having had little if any exposure to images of Africa and Africans that were anything other than a negation of the West and of "civilization" itself, was best left in the jungle. As exaggerated as it may sound in an era of recuperation of both the slave past and the African past, that summarizes much of the Black middle class's attitude to both around the turn of the century and even through the 1920s.

If we can generalize, the New Negroes initially believed that, through individual agency, they could escape the clutches of the laws and social practices that sought both to confine all Black people under the same second-class-citizen status and define all Black people, regardless of class or difference, as Black—as the same.

This nexus of respectability versus disrespectability, the high arts versus folklore, and the past versus the present is epitomized by the work of two very different men: the white author Joel Chandler Harris and the Black author Charles W. Chesnutt.[25]

Joel Chandler Harris and his creation Uncle Remus changed the fate of Black folklore. It is safe to say that Uncle Remus was the most popular Black literary character in all of American history. Harris's enormous commercial success could not help but draw comment from Black writers and readers and tempt some to attempt to replicate what he had done, but from within their own Black aesthetic.

No one was more successful at recuperating the Negro

folk tradition from the "plantation tradition" than Charles W. Chesnutt, whose stories subverted the tendency among some white folklorists to romanticize antebellum life in the South and render the relations between enslavers and the enslaved in metaphors of consanguinity such as "aunties" and "uncles."

Chesnutt burst onto the American literary scene with the publication of his first short story, "The Goophered Grapevine," in *The Atlantic Monthly*, in August 1887[26]— incidentally, the same year the term "New Negro" first appeared in print. Chesnutt was the first Black author to appear in those pages, eleven years after Joel Chandler Harris had introduced Uncle Remus to the American reading public in *The Atlanta Constitution* and seven years after *Uncle Remus: His Songs and His Sayings* was published as a book. Chesnutt was very aware of the relationship of his fictional Black character, Julius McAdoo, to Uncle Remus, and of his own relationship to Harris. These were relationships of repetition and reversal, or signifying. Uncle Julius is a trickster figure whose Remus-like demeanor fools the white male northerner who narrates the stories, which offer realistic depictions of the brutalities of the "slave regime," as Frederick Douglass called it, as well as revelations of ingenious uses of "conjuration" to rescue enslaved people from those brutalities.

Chesnutt collected seven of his stories and published

them as *The Conjure Woman* in 1899, to great critical acclaim, if not financial success.[27] He was keenly aware of the stakes of his aesthetic project; as he wrote in a fascinating essay, "Superstitions and Folk-lore of the South" (1901), he "embodied into a number of stories" the "old-time belief in what was known as 'conjuration' or 'goopher,'" a set of practices "brought over from the dark continent by the dark people," the enslaved Africans, and "certain features [of which] suggest a distant affinity with Voodooism, or snake worship, a cult which seems to have been indigenous," he concludes erroneously, "to tropical America."[28] Here Chesnutt has staked a claim for the cultural continuities between African and New World African cultures, and he valorized the slave experience that fused them together: "In the old plantation days they flourished vigorously, though discouraged by the 'great house,' and their potency was well established among the blacks and the poorer whites."[29] Chesnutt also wrote about Harris as late as 1931, in his important essay "Post-Bellum Pre-Harlem."[30]

If the ghost of enslavement haunted attitudes among the Black middle class about Black folklore and its related idiomatic forms, the shadows of Joel Chandler Harris (whom, as Sterling A. Brown reminded us, the philosopher Alain Locke damned as "a kindly amanuensis for the illiterate Negro peasant")[31] fell over Chesnutt's work (as his silent second text) and over subsequent estimations of the nature and function of African American folklore in general. As Brown put it in 1950, four years after the release of Disney's classic *Song of the South* (in which James Baskett, as Remus, consoles a lonely little white boy, played by Bobby Driscoll, with tales of that wily trickster, Brer Rabbit): "One thing made clear by the resurrection of Uncle Remus in Walt Disney's *Song of the South* is the degree to which he belonged to white people rather than to the Negro folk."[32] At the same time, however, Brown is quick to point to the importance of Harris to the preservation of Black folklore: "Whether familiarity has bred contempt, or whether there has been too great a sensitivity toward folk expression, Negroes have lagged behind whites in the gathering of folk tales. Without Joel Chandler Harris, it is likely that the Uncle Remus stories, which now belong with the minor masterpieces of American literature, would have been lost."[33] Brown lamented the fact that "educated Negroes by and large have not been greatly interested,"[34] despite having concluded in 1941 that "awareness of the importance of a study of the folk is increasing among Negroes, but still slowly."[35]

But the problem with Harris was as much ideological as it was literary: his representation of slavery, through Remus, was part of the larger attempt to reclaim slavery as a golden age in the history of American race relations, a process that unfolded precisely as the effects of Reconstruction were being rolled back and Jim Crow segregation was being legislated and legitimized. In this dreadful process, Negro folklore had been summoned, dressed in the clothes and voicing the words of the ever-loyal, always-faithful, grateful servant, Uncle Remus, something of a distant family member but in blackface. As Brown puts it, "The stark and almost cynical qualities of genuine folklore, especially that of rural Negroes, are deleted in favor of gentility and sentiment. . . . [T]heir purpose was more to cast a golden glow over the antebellum South than to set forth authentic Negro folklore."[36]

But, Brown argues, we should not allow the denuding of the essence of Negro folklore by apologists for slavery, such as Harris, to deter us from collecting and nourishing the folk tradition. For in these tales, just as in the spirituals, is embedded the first expression of the aesthetic foundation of African American culture.

There is no more pointed example of this New Negro resistance to the presumed equation of race and class than in the novel *The Marrow of Tradition* (1901). Chesnutt narrates from the perspective of a Black doctor sent to the "Black car" after riding in the "white car" with a fellow white doctor:

They were noisy, loquacious, happy, dirty, and malodorous. For a while Miller was amused and pleased. They were his people, and he felt a certain expansive warmth toward them in spite of their obvious shortcomings. By and by, however, the air became too close, and he went out upon the platform. For the sake of the democratic ideal, which meant so much to his race, he might have endured the affliction. He could easily imagine that people of refinement, with the power in their hands, might be tempted to strain the democratic ideal in order to avoid such contact, but . . . these people were just as offensive to him as to the whites in the other end of the train. Surely if a classification of passengers on trains was at all desirable, it might be made of some more logical and considerate basis than a mere arbitrary, tactless, and by the very nature of things, brutal drawing of a color line.[37]

The New Negroes, often through the politics of respectability, trumpeted their class difference within the race in an attempt to make the case that they should be treated differently than lower-class Black people, with whom they had little in common. Of course we now know that this strategy didn't work, and by 1909, when Du Bois joined a few other Black people and several wealthy white liberals to form the National Association for the Advancement of Colored People (NAACP), the Black upper class, by and large, knew it, too.

Du Bois famously said that all races "are saved by [their] exceptional men."[38] But what is curious is that even in *The Souls of Black Folk*, which became instantly famous for his critique of Booker T. Washington's accommodationism, Du Bois himself endorsed restriction of the right to vote among the poor. "The alternative thus offered the nation," he writes in *Souls*, "was not between full and restricted Negro suffrage; else every sensible man, Black and white, would easily have chosen the latter."[39] In other words, even the radical Du Bois, at least in 1903, saw voting as a privilege of the Talented Tenth.

Du Bois had foreshadowed this belief in differentiating the treatment of Black social classes in his classic of American sociology, *The Philadelphia Negro* (1899): "The colored people are seldom judged by their best classes, and often the very existence of classes among them is ignored. . . . If the Negroes were by themselves[,] either a strong aristocratic system or a dictatorship would for the present prevail. With, however, democracy thus prematurely thrust upon them, the first impulse of the best, the wisest and richest is to segregate themselves from the mass. . . . [I]t is just as natural for the well-educated and well-to-do Negroes to feel themselves far above the criminals and prostitutes of Seventh and Lombard streets, and even above the servant girls and porters of the middle class of workers. So far they are justified. . . ."[40]

David Levering Lewis argues that it was only the fact that the color curtain, with its social discrimination and political disfranchisement, ultimately came down as hard on the Black elite as it had on the Black poor that forced the Black elite to stop conceiving of itself as somehow separate.[41] It was a class-blind form of Black oppression more than anything else that cemented unity in the race. As Du Bois concluded in the same paragraph from *The Philadelphia Negro*, "So far they are justified; but they make their mistake in failing to recognize that however laudable an ambition to rise may be, the first duty of an upper class is to serve the lowest classes. The aristocracies of all peoples have been slow in learning this and perhaps the Negro is no slower than the rest, but his peculiar situation demands that in his case this lesson be learned sooner."[42]

Just over 10 percent of Black people were free by 1860, which may be the source of the idea of the Talented Tenth in the first place. Just like the yawning class divide between the Black community and the white community, the Black class structure has always been skewed in this country, and, contrary to our expectations in the civil rights and Black Power movements, that internal class divide has not changed to the present day, despite the tremendous gains of so many of us who were able to take advantage of affirmative action education and employment opportunities. I say "so many of us," but of course that is also to say *not nearly enough of us.* Is the success of one class within the Black community at the expense of the other? Du Bois's entire oeuvre grapples with the idea that Blacks are one yet not one, that we rise and fall together even as some of us rise to the greatest heights.

CHAPTER FIVE

The "True Art of a Race's Past"

ART, PROPAGANDA, AND THE NEW NEGRO

The Harlem Renaissance was a period in the 1920s during which the creation of literature and art became a crucial part of the quest for civil rights; W. E. B. Du Bois's biographer David Levering Lewis would call it "civil rights by copyright."[1] The roots of the Harlem Renaissance can be traced to the last decade of the nineteenth century, and one woman in particular, Victoria Earle Matthews, played an outsize role. Matthews is the link between the discourse on race during the Enlightenment and the decades of the 1840s and '50s, and what became in the 1920s the Harlem or "New Negro" Renaissance.

Matthews was born Victoria Earle in 1861 in Fort Valley,

Georgia. Her mother, Caroline Smith, was enslaved; it is possible that Victoria's father was her mother's enslaver. Caroline escaped to New York during the Civil War and returned to retrieve her family around 1873. The family then moved to New York City. Young Victoria studied at Grammar School 48 but had to leave because her family couldn't afford to continue her education. She worked as a domestic servant while maintaining her own private studies. At age eighteen she married William Matthews, and the couple had one son. Their marriage was not a happy one.[2]

Matthews was a prolific writer. She contributed to major newspapers, including *The New York Times*, and was a correspondent for the Black publications *The New York Age*, *The Washington Bee*, and the *Richmond Planet*. She also wrote biographical essays for the *New York Weekly*, *Waverly Magazine*, and *Family Story Paper*. She published the story "Aunt Lindy: A Story Founded on Real Life" in the *AME Church Review* in 1889.[3]

Matthews was also an organizer. In 1892 she cofounded with Maritcha Lyons and other prominent Black women the Woman's Loyal Union of New York and Brooklyn, to protest lynching and to support Ida B. Wells, who thanked the women for helping to fund her pamphlet *Southern Horrors*. The historian Val Marie Johnson calls the Woman's Loyal Union "an organizational springboard to the National Association of Colored Women," which had its roots at the inaugural National Conference of Colored Women, convened by Josephine St. Pierre Ruffin in Boston in July 1895. Out of this conference was formed the National Federation of Afro-American Women, which merged with another group, the National League of Colored Women, to form the National Association of Colored Women (NACW) in 1896. Matthews was appointed chair of the executive board of the NACW.[4]

It was at this Boston conference that Matthews delivered her influential essay "The Value of Race Literature" as an address. The piece begins with an epigraph from Ralph Waldo Emerson: "If the black man carries in his bosom an indispensable element of a new and coming civilization, for the sake of that element, no money, nor strength, nor circumstance can hurt him; he will survive and play his part. . . . If you have *man*, black or white is an insignificance. The intellect—that is miraculous!"[5]

Emerson thus believed that intellectual and artistic production could offset color prejudice. Matthews argued that this production was happening in the form of literature: "What is bright, hopeful and encouraging is in reality the source of an original school of race literature, of racial psychology, of potent possibilities, an amalgam needed for this great American race of the future."[6]

Along with Emerson, Matthews also points to Antonín Dvořák, the classical composer who, from 1892 to

1895, was the director of the National Conservatory of Music in New York City. While there, he met Harry Burleigh, a Black student and soloist at the elite, otherwise all-white St. George's Episcopal Church. Burleigh introduced Dvořák to the spirituals. In 1893, inspired by these Sorrow Songs, as Du Bois called them, Dvořák composed his most famous piece of music, Symphony no. 9, *From the New World*, which would become recognized by some as the greatest original work of American classical music. "I am now satisfied," Dvořák said, "that the future music of this continent must be founded upon what are called the Negro melodies. . . . In the Negro melodies of America I discover all that is needed for a great and noble school of music. They are pathetic, tender, passionate, and melancholy, solemn, religious, bold, merry, gay, gracious, or what you will. It is music that suits itself to any work or any purpose. There is nothing in the whole range of composition that cannot find a thematic source here."[7] In quoting Dvořák's interview from the May 21, 1893, edition of the Sunday *New York Herald*, Matthews altered a word here and there, but the meaning was unchanged.

Matthews uses Dvořák's claims about the originality of Black American music to support her call for a new race literature, created by African American people and out of the same wellspring of experience that had influenced the Negro spirituals. "A Race Literature," she wrote, is "a necessity to dissipate the odium conjured up by the term 'colored' persons." The experiences of Black people and the fight against racism are "the source of an original school of race literature, of racial psychology, of potent possibilities" for the progress of the race and therefore the end of racism.[8]

Prefiguring an argument that James Weldon Johnson would make in 1922, when he would call for what became the Harlem Renaissance, Matthews summoned the examples of two great Black foreign writers to show that through literature, a Black person could overcome racial prejudice: Alexander Pushkin, universally hailed as the father of Russian literature (he was killed in a duel in 1837), whose mother's mother's father was a Black African; and Alexandre Dumas, the author of the extraordinarily popular novels *The Count of Monte Cristo* and *The Three Musketeers*, both published in 1844, the same year that Emerson delivered his speech. Dumas's father's mother was a Haitian of mixed African and French ancestry. Both Pushkin and Dumas, biracial but Black, like Frederick Douglass, had shown that great achievement— and success with white audiences—was possible.

Matthews argues that this new, elevated race literature ("an outlet for the unnaturally suppressed inner lives which our people have been compelled to lead") would "drive out the traditional Negro in dialect,—the subordinate, the servant as the type representing a 'race' whose numbers are now far into the millions," the "typical Darkey" stereotype so frequently depicted in minstrelsy, on the vaudeville stage, and in Sambo images—a character, Matthews says, that signifies "cowardice, self-negation and lack of responsibility." In other words, Matthews seems to agree that there was some truth in stereotypes of the Old Negro. Depictions of a New Negro, in her view, could be used to further the cause of the Black middle and upper classes in their battle to protect at least their own rights as citizens, even if they couldn't protect the rights of the Black masses.[9]

Here again is evidence of the great political importance of literature. Since the Enlightenment, we have seen the persuasiveness of writing in debates about the African's place in nature; some of these arguments were, of course, virulently racist, as in the case of Kant and Jefferson. These arguments continued to influence agitation to abolish slavery, right up through the abolitionist movement's discovery of the power of the testimony of formerly enslaved persons such as Frederick Douglass in the genre of the slave narratives, as attested by that powerful speech of Emerson's that Victoria Earle Matthews quoted. Incidentally, Emerson had delivered that speech at an antislavery rally in Concord, Massachusetts, in 1844, with Frederick Douglass sitting on the stage behind him.

. . .

Daniel A. P. Murray, the first Black assistant librarian of Congress, said, "The true test of the progress of a people is to be found in their literature."[10] The first New Negro Literary Renaissance began around the same time that Du Bois deployed photography as a weapon in the war to redefine the image of the New Negro in his exhibition at the Paris Exposition in 1900. In that same year, the original New Negro, Booker T. Washington, published *A New Negro for a New Century*, a book containing essays about the phenomenon by various Black authors, including his soon-to-be nemesis, Du Bois. A year later, in 1901, the Black Boston literary critic William Stanley Braithwaite declared, "We are at the commencement of a 'negroid' renaissance . . . that will have in time as much importance in literary history as the much spoken of and much praised Celtic and Canadian renaissance."[11]

Three years later, in an essay entitled "The New Negro Literary Movement," published in *The African Methodist Episcopal Church Review*, William H. A. Moore said that the works of three great Black writers—the poems of Paul Laurence Dunbar, *The Souls of Black Folk* by W. E. B. Du Bois, and the novels and short stories of Charles W. Chesnutt—were already of such a high quality that they constituted the renaissance that Braithwaite had anticipated. Claims about this New Negro Literary Movement unfolded alongside new articles about the nature of "The New Negro Man" and "The New Negro Woman," both published in that same year, 1904, in *The Voice of the Negro* magazine.

The metaphor of the New Negro was a powerful construct, like an empty vessel or signifier that different—and even contradictory—ideologies, such as Black nationalism and socialism, could (and would) fill for their own political or propagandistic purposes. It is important to note that these various New Negro movements between 1900 and 1925 occurred against the backdrop of the Great Migration, when millions of poor, Black, rural, agrarian sharecroppers came flooding into cities in the South and then into industrial centers in the North, creating two distinct classes of Black people in urban areas. In fact, the size of the Black population in the North between 1910 and 1930 almost tripled, going from 484,176 in 1910 to 1,146,985 in 1930.[12]

New York City's Harlem wasn't always the Black mecca that James Weldon Johnson would later anoint it. In 1910, it was still an overwhelmingly white community: Of its total population of 181,949, 90.01 percent were white and 9.89 percent Black. A decade later, in 1920, Harlem was still primarily white, but the numbers were changing. With a total population of 216,026 people, it was now just 67.47 percent white. But by 1930, during the Harlem

Renaissance, Harlem, with a total population of 209,663, had flipped (and actually dropped), becoming 70.18 percent Black and only 29.43 percent white. The Black population grew as a result of the migration of poor Black people from the South, along with, to a lesser extent, migrants from the Caribbean.[13]

As the writings of Chesnutt and Du Bois showed, Black people whose families had lived in the North for generations did not always welcome poor Black southerners. The self-defined New Negroes viewed themselves as a northern cosmopolitan elite that could integrate into American society, whereas "the slow moving black masses" (as the National Urban League's research director Charles S. Johnson, the first Black person to earn a PhD in sociology from the University of Chicago, along with Alain Locke, one of the proverbial "midwives" of the New Negro Renaissance, would actually call them) could not.[14] In other words, the New Negro Movement was about class, about class differences within the Black community.

But it was also about politics. The metaphor of the New Negro reemerged as a more explicitly political concept in the late teens. By the end of World War I, the Black socialist movement had seized upon the metaphor to declare a new day in American history, where Black people fought their oppressors with guns, inspired by the fact that Black men had served in the war and had been treated equally by white people in Europe. Why should they return after risking their lives and take Jim Crow racism lying down? To the socialists, led by A. Philip Randolph, the New Negro was a warrior: "to fight back in self defense, should be accepted as a matter of course."[15] Everybody else was an Old Negro, including Du Bois, Washington, and Marcus Garvey.

Yet Garvey, the father of the Back to Africa movement, also presented himself as a New Negro. "The New Negro," Garvey said in a speech in October 1919, in the aftermath of the bloody "Red Summer," "backed by the Universal Negro Improvement Association is determined to restore Africa to the world, and you scattered children of Africa in Newport News, you children of Ethiopia, I want you to understand that the call is now made to you. What are you going to do? . . . [A]re you going to link up your strength, morally and financially, with the other Negroes of the world and let us all fight one battle unto victory?" The choice, in Garvey's view, was liberty or death. "The war must go on; only that the war is not going on in France or Flanders, but the war will go on in the African plains, there to decide once and for all in the very near future whether Black men are to be serfs and slaves or Black men are to be free."[16]

The leaders of the race, including James Weldon Johnson, feared the militancy of the Black socialists and of

Marcus Garvey's Black cultural and political nationalists. Nevertheless, they took the New Negro concept as their own, stripping it of its explicitly political content and transforming it into an artistic movement that they thought could achieve an implicit political effect.

The National Urban League's Johnson; Alain Locke, who earned three degrees from Harvard, including the first PhD ever awarded to a Black person in philosophy, and who was the first Black Rhodes Scholar; and the great Du Bois, representing the NAACP, decided to work together to wage the war against anti-Black racism on an entirely different front from those advocated by the socialist New Negroes and the Garveyite New Negroes. Art would prove the Negro's intellectual equality, the Negro's claim to the natural rights of man.

These leaders in the early 1920s called for a "New Negro Renaissance," a renaissance that would be based in Harlem, which had become by 1925 the capital of the Negro world, at least in a cultural sense. James Weldon Johnson enshrined the image of the Black mecca in his book *Black Manhattan*. On the topic of race literature, Johnson, in the preface to his 1922 *Book of American Negro Poetry*, echoed Victoria Earle Matthews:

> A people may become great through many means, but there is only one measure by which its great-

ness is recognized and acknowledged. The final measure of the greatness of all peoples is the amount and standard of the literature and art they have produced. The world does not know that a people is great until that people produces great literature and art. No people that has produced great literature and art has ever been looked upon by the world as distinctly inferior.

The status of the Negro in the United States is more a question of national mental attitude toward the race than of actual condition. And nothing will do more to change that mental attitude and raise his status than a demonstration of intellectual parity by the Negro through the production of literature and art.[17]

Johnson's words turned out to be a rallying cry.

The Harlem Renaissance was officially born in the form of a massive, widely heralded and reviewed anthology called *The New Negro*, edited by Alain Locke and published with color illustrations in 1925. The National Urban League and the NAACP, through their magazines *Opportunity* and *The Crisis*, began organizing competitions, with cash prizes awarded at glitzy black-tie dinners in New York at which the country's most famous white writers and publishers gathered to honor its most famous Black writers and artists, such as Langston Hughes, Jean Toomer, Countee Cullen, and Zora Neale Hurston.

It was a heady time. Hughes said that Negroes created

art and literature as if their lives depended on it. But he also would later write that if there was a renaissance, the average Black person in Harlem never heard about it.

Therein lies the problem. The Harlem Renaissance produced some of the greatest Black writers and artists in the history of the African American literary tradition, including several, like Claude McKay, who migrated to Harlem from the West Indies, and it would later inspire a new generation of writers in the sixties in the Black Arts Movement. The Renaissance also encouraged Black artists to look to Africa as a source of artistic inspiration, when even many Black people largely ascribed to the same stereotypes of Africa in which white people believed. Still, for the writers of the Harlem Renaissance, African art never became a structuring principle. Rather, it remained on the surface, a theme, like putting palm trees and cowrie shells in the background of a landscape. Africa, for these Black men and women, was a source of imagery, the home of the tom-tom drum. Take, for instance, Countee Cullen's poem "Heritage":

> What is Africa to me:
> Copper sun or scarlet sea,
> Jungle star or jungle track,
> Strong bronzed men, or regal Black
> Women from whose loins I sprang

When the birds of Eden sang?
One three centuries removed
From the scenes his fathers loved,
Spicy grove and cinnamon tree,
What is Africa to me?[18]

This mode of representation is called "primitivism." Duke Ellington's name for his original jazz band was the Jungle Band, and there was the famous Jungle Alley in Harlem, a nightclub row on 133rd Street. In Josephine Baker's "Revue Negres" routine in Paris, she played an African princess living in the jungle, dressed solely in a ring of very phallic bananas. Africa remained a fad, even a fashion statement, for the Harlem Renaissance artists, something they were "of" or "from," but never "in." Very few of these Black artists even visited Africa. (Then again, neither did Marcus Garvey.)

The lofty goals of the Renaissance, however, had no chance. Art has never liberated a people. Shakespeare's creative output was supported by the economic and political power of Elizabethan England, which followed England's stunning victory over the Spanish Armada in 1588. *Hamlet* didn't liberate England; England, you might say, liberated Shakespeare and *Hamlet*. Pushkin emerged from the stability and prosperity produced by Peter the Great, the very same emperor who purchased and enslaved Pushkin's

African great-grandfather, then freed him and made him a general.

The Harlem Renaissance, consisting as it did of perhaps some fifty writers and artists, in reality aimed to create a vanguard of elite writers and intellectuals. Du Bois himself rendered this judgment of the significance and limitations of the Renaissance at the annual conference of the NAACP in June 1926, the year after the white journalist Heywood Broun, the keynote speaker at the New York Urban League literary dinner in 1925, had made the ridiculous claim that only through the coming of a Black Shakespeare or a Black Dante would the race ever be truly liberated. Du Bois bluntly told these same writers who had been in the audience, by and large, when Broun had spoken the year before, "We have, to be sure, a few recognized and successful Negro artists; but they are not all those fit to survive or even a good minority."[19]

Du Bois did not name these artists or their works. I would say that *Cane*, published by Jean Toomer in 1923, is a masterpiece; *The Weary Blues* and *Fine Clothes to the Jew*, by a young Langston Hughes, and *God's Trombones*, by James Weldon Johnson, are also unrivaled examples of the successful transformation of vernacular forms into a formal literary poetic diction, just as James Weldon Johnson had called for in his manifesto of 1922. Other similarly innovative texts, such as Sterling Brown's *Southern Road*, published in 1931, and Zora Neale Hurston's *Their Eyes Were Watching God*, in 1937, were created after the Renaissance had ended, but are extensions, intertextual riffs, on the techniques that Hughes and Johnson pioneered. Other critics, of course, will have their list of works produced during the decade of the 1920s that were sophisticated aesthetic achievements.

Du Bois cited three reasons for the artistic limitations of the Harlem Renaissance. First, not enough Black artists had overcome their ambivalent feelings about Black history: "that past, of which for long years we have been ashamed, for which we have apologized. We thought nothing good could come out of that past which we wanted to remember, which we wanted to hand down to our children." But, he admitted, "in a half shamefaced way, we are beginning to be proud of it."

Second, Du Bois criticized the very premise of the Renaissance, that its chief political impact could only be realized if its writers created a nonpolitical art; that civil rights as art will be more effective than civil rights as politics.

> They are whispering, "Here is a way out. Here is the real solution of the color problem. The recognition accorded Cullen, Hughes, Fauset, White

and others shows there is no real color line. Keep quiet! Don't complain! Work! All will be well!" I will not say that already this chorus amounts to a conspiracy. Perhaps I am naturally too suspicious. But I will say that there are today a surprising number of white people who are getting great satisfaction out of these younger Negro writers because they think it is going to stop agitation of the Negro question.

These people, Du Bois continues, only want Black art created, in his words, by "Uncle Toms, Topsies, good 'darkies,' and clowns."

And third, Du Bois said, "We are ashamed"—ashamed of being Black, ashamed of ourselves, ashamed of revealing our full humanity in the way that Black vernacular culture does. The Black middle class, he continued, is ashamed "of sex and we lower our eyes when people talk of it. Our religion holds us in superstition. Our worst side has been so shamelessly emphasized that we are denying we have or ever had a worst side. In all sorts of ways," Du Bois concludes, "we are hemmed in" by the choice of subject matter and language, and so "our new young artists have got to fight their way to freedom,"[20] which to him, writing at the height of the Harlem Renaissance, these writers had not yet done.

JAZZ: "NEGRO—AND BEAUTIFUL"

In my view, the most formally original Black artists of the 1920s were not to be found primarily among the writers or painters but among jazz musicians. Their art incorporated both Black folklore and Black vernacular traditions, emerging from the underground, the same place from which "Shine and the *Titanic*" and "The Signifying Monkey" emerged, from the streets of lower-class Black communities, in the cabarets, speakeasies, and juke joints. It was born before the very eyes, or under the noses and feet and ears, of the Harlem Renaissance intellectuals and writers, too many of whom were so intent upon pleasing both real and imaginary middle-class white patrons and readers that they were deaf to the sounds of this astonishing artistic revolution around them.

Langston Hughes was one of the few Renaissance writers who understood jazz's potential to serve as the foundation of a new aesthetic for Black literary forms, especially in the creation of a new poetic diction, as he sought, quite successfully I believe, to demonstrate in his first two books of poetry. He expressed this point eloquently—and controversially—in his essay "The Negro Artist and the Racial Mountain," his retort to then-radical journalist

George Schuyler's essay "The Negro-Art Hokum," both published in *The Nation* in 1926.

While Schuyler noted the creation of jazz (as well as other vernacular forms such as the spirituals, the blues, and the Charleston), he argues that "these are contributions of a caste in a certain section of the country. They are foreign," he maintains, "to Northern Negroes, West Indian Negroes, and African Negroes." In other words, he continues, these are the artistic products of "the peasantry of the South" and are not in any way "expressive or characteristic of the Negro race." They are regional and class-based artistic expressions, not ethnic at all, or only incidentally. He concludes "the Aframerican is merely a lamp-blacked Anglo-Saxon," fundamentally the same in every significant way as his white neighbor. For Schuyler, "environment," "nationality," and "education" trump race every time, since, as he puts it, "your American Negro is just plain American." And as for the so-called "great renaissance of Negro art just around the corner waiting to be ushered on the scene" in which "new art forms [would be developed] expressing the 'peculiar' psychology of the Negro," he says devastatingly. "Skeptics patiently waited. They still wait."[21]

Hughes defended jazz fiercely:

> Jazz is to me one of the inherent expressions of Negro life in America: the eternal tom-tom beat-

ing in the Negro soul . . . the tom-tom of revolt against weariness in a white world, a world of subway trains, and work, work, work; the tom-tom of joy and laughter, and pain swallowed in a smile. Yet the Philadelphia clubwoman [sometimes thought to be a dig at Alain Locke's famously conservative mother] is ashamed to say that her race created it and she does not like me to write about it. The old subconscious "white is best" runs through her mind. Years of study under white teachers, a lifetime of white books, pictures, and papers, and white manners, morals, and Puritan standards made her dislike the spirituals. And now she turns up her nose at jazz and all its manifestations—likewise almost everything else distinctly racial. . . . She wants . . . to make the white world believe that all Negroes are as smug and as near white in soul as she wants to be. But to my mind, it is the duty of the younger Negro artist . . . to change through the force of his art that old whispering "I want to be white," hidden in the aspirations of his people, to "Why should I want to be white? I am a Negro—and beautiful."[22]

But Hughes's was a minority voice at best—one that, at least in their aesthetic writings, the older shapers of taste and patronage in the Renaissance could not or would not hear. "Let the blare of Negro jazz bands and the bellowing voice of Bessie Smith singing Blues," Hughes concludes, "penetrate the closed ears of the colored near-intellectuals until they listen and perhaps understand." Let these sublime artists, he says, "cause the smug Negro middle class to turn from their white, respectable, ordinary books and papers to catch a glimmer of their own beauty."[23]

The New Negro anthology contained only one essay on jazz, "Jazz at Home" by the autodidact Joel A. Rogers, and it said essentially that because jazz "vulgarizes," it needed what he called "more wholesome growth" to reach its full potential. Therefore, he concludes, we had to "try to lift and divert it into nobler channels."[24]

FOLKLORE: TELLING AND RETELLING

This attitude is similar to those found in debates at the time about the collection and preservation of Negro folklore.[25] After all, were the Brer Rabbit and Brer Bear stories remnants of the ignorance and primitivism of illiterate enslaved people, or were they worthy of collection, study, and admiration? This debate coincided with questions over the relation of the American Negro to Africa. Was the Black American an "African" American, or did the dreadful, harsh, and deadly Middle Passage erase Africa from the enslaved person's memory?

The debate was not new. On May 25, 1894, as part of

a program hosted by the Hampton Folklore Society, the pioneering Black scholar Anna Julia Cooper delivered remarks at the Hampton Normal School (now Hampton University) that were almost certainly the first to be made by a Black feminist intellectual arguing for the importance of Negro folklore. Her remarks would prove prescient in defining the terms of the debate about the nature and function of this body of oral lore and its relation to the social progress and political status of an emergent people just twenty-nine years "up from slavery." In her lecture, printed in the July edition of the *Southern Workman* monthly magazine, Cooper cleverly cast the heart of her argument for preserving Negro folklore in terms of "originality":

> Emancipation from the model is what is needed. Servile copying foredooms mediocrity: it cuts the nerve of soul expression. The American Negro cannot produce an original utterance until he realizes the sanctity of his homely inheritance. . . . The creative instinct must be aroused by a wholesome respect for the thoughts that lie nearest. And this to my mind is the vital importance for him of the study of his own folk-lore. His songs, superstitions, customs, tales, are the legacy left from the imagery of the past. These must catch and hold and work up into the pictures he paints. . . . The Negro too is a painter.

Rarely could a bolder argument for the nature and function of African American folklore have been made, and Cooper was making this argument just less than a year after the appearance of what would become, after its debut in the December 1893 number, a regular column on "Folklore and Ethnology" in the pages of the magazine. Just that November, the first Negro folklore society had been formed at Hampton, under the direction of a farseeing white administrator there, Alice M. Bacon, as a branch of the American Folklore Society, which itself had launched in 1888. Students and alumni were asked to contribute examples of traditional Negro folklore to the journal, which encouraged them to transcribe tales they remembered or encountered. Accordingly, *The Southern Workman*, at the turn of the century and well into the twentieth, became a living archive or laboratory of Negro folklore, and its readers became its informants, its documentarians.

Cooper's advocacy for the crucial importance of collecting Negro folklore may seem at odds with the movement for the "politics of respectability," with its ardent call to eschew (in manners, habits, demeanor, comportment, and especially in spoken English) the slave past, even as attempts were being made to preserve the former slave's cultural heritage. But, as the anthropologist Lee D. Baker explains, Alice M. Bacon and other key figures in the rise of the Hampton Folklore Society believed that by collecting Negro folklore, they could measure the progress African Americans had achieved, with the aid of institutions like Hampton, since Emancipation, while also preserving the unique traces of a cultural legacy that reached back through enslavement to Africa. "The educators and graduates of Hampton Normal and Agricultural Institute," Baker writes in *Anthropology and the Racial Politics of Culture* (2010), "formed the society to salvage and record cultural practices of rural blacks to demonstrate that industrial education succeeded in fostering the so-called Christian civilization of its graduates—in part by using folklore to evaluate how much African heritage remained to be rooted out."[26] On the one hand, then, a certain segment of the African American community saw Negro folklore, like dialect, as a discursive remnant of slavery, a cultural and a social embarrassment, best left behind in the antebellum South. On the other hand, Baker explains, Cooper's comments revealed "that even at the formation of the first black folklore society, some African Americans understood that folklore could provide a positive interpretation of their African heritage or a scientific basis to identify and preserve their distinctive culture."[27]

By the 1920s, three decades after Cooper presented her

incisive remarks, collecting Negro folklore had become commonplace, though not without its controversies. Several important volumes were published during the twenties, including Thomas W. Talley's *Negro Folk Rhymes (Wise and Otherwise)* in 1922 and Elsie Clews Parsons's *Folk-Lore of the Sea Islands, South Carolina* in 1923.[28] Parsons was a champion for the collection of Negro folklore, commissioning and guest-editing fourteen issues of *The Journal of American Folklore* dedicated to African and African American folklore in her capacity as the journal's associate editor. In 1925, the pioneering Black anthropologist Arthur Huff Fauset published "Negro Folk Tales from the South (Alabama, Mississippi, Louisiana)" in *The New Negro*,[29] followed in 1931 by *Black Gods of the Metropolis*.[30]

In his essay in *The New Negro*, Fauset stressed the need for the African American community to preserve a wider and more authentic variety of Negro folklore than the tales popularized by—and in part, he argued, distorted by—Joel Chandler Harris. He also compiled an essential bibliography of folk materials for the book. Fauset knew that the status of Black folklore was a highly charged subject among Black critics and writers. He argued, first, that Negro folklore was "based upon the original folk tales of the African slaves,"[31] itself a contentious claim, one fraught with danger for those who would be dubious about the status of the cultures created by Black people in Africa and who passionately argued that the submerged position of the American Negro in American society was the result of the harmful effects of slavery, having nothing at all to do with the place of Africa and Africans on the scale of world civilization. Further, they believed that associations with Africa effectively dragged the position of the American Negro downward.[32]

Fauset went on to argue for the salient effects of valorizing Negro folklore, precisely at this crucial time when Black writers were using culture, especially the written and oral verbal arts, as prima facie evidence that Black people were intellectually equal to white people and hence entitled to the full rights and privileges of American citizenship:

> The great storehouse from which they were gleaned, that treasury of folk lore which the American Negro inherited from his African forefathers, is little known. It rivals in amount as well as in quality that of any people on the face of the globe, and is not confined to stories of the Uncle Remus type, but includes a wide variety of story forms, legends, saga cycles, songs, proverbs and phantastic, almost mythical material. . . . It is not necessary to draw upon sentiment in order to realize the masterful quality of some of the Negro tales: it is simply necessary to read them. . . . The antiquity and the authentic folk lore ancestry of the Negro tale make it the proper subject for the scientific folk-lorist rather than the literary amateur [such as

Joel Chandler Harris, whom he cites earlier]. It is
the ethnologist, the philologist, and the student of
primitive psychology that are most needed for its
present investigation.[33]

In an essay published in 1965, titled "Why I Returned,"
Arna Bontemps pointed to the place of African American
folklore as a trope and placeholder in a larger battle that
had raged within the Black middle class about "roots,"
origins, vernacular culture, modernism, cultural identity,
and social mobility since the politics-of-respectability debates that, as we have seen, surfaced in the 1890s and continued through the Harlem Renaissance of the 1920s and
well beyond.

Bontemps is quite eloquent about the way that diamet-
rically opposed opinions about the life or death of Black
vernacular culture could manifest themselves at the dinner table and divide families into two distinct camps:

> In their opposing attitudes towards roots, my fa-
> ther and my great-uncle made me aware of a con-
> flict in which every educated American Negro,
> and some who are not educated, must somehow
> take sides. By implication at least, one group advo-
> cates embracing the riches of the folk heritage;
> their opposites demand a clean break with the past
> and all it represents. Had I not gone home sum-
> mers and hob-nobbed with folk-type Negroes, I
> would have finished college without knowing that

any Negro other than Paul Laurence Dunbar ever wrote a poem. I would have come out imagining that the story of the Negro could be told in two short paragraphs: a statement about jungle people in Africa and an equally brief account of the slavery issue in American history.[34]

The conflict over aesthetics, cultural "authenticity," and the relation of Black Americans to their African cultural forebears would simmer through the Harlem Renaissance and perhaps reach its zenith in the late 1930s and early 1940s, during the famous, heated debate between the sociologist E. Franklin Frazier and the anthropologist Melville J. Herskovits.

In his essay "The Negro's Americanism," published in *The New Negro*,[35] Herskovits maintained that the American Negro was sui generis, culturally; that there was no "Africa" remaining in African American cultural and social institutions, because the Middle Passage and slavery had effectively obliterated any remnants of Africa even in African American vernacular culture. But by 1930, he had begun to approach the matter with more nuance, positing what we might think of as a sliding scale of Africanism among Black peoples in the New World, ranging from "the Bush Negroes of Suriname who exhibit a civilization which is most African" to Negro Americans in the North, "a group where, to all intents and purposes, there is nothing of the African tradition left, [and] . . . who only differ from their white neighbors in the fact that they have more pigmentation in their skins." He argues that evidence for the relation between African and African American culture resides in "folklore, religion, and music."[36]

By 1941, Herskovits had completely reversed his initial position, and powerfully so, adopting the stance earlier articulated by his doctoral adviser at Columbia University, Franz Boas, whose disagreement with the seminal University of Chicago sociologist Robert E. Park over the presence of African survivals in African American culture was an important precursor to the Herskovits-Frazier debate. (Frazier had studied with Park at Chicago before heading up the sociology department at Howard University in Washington, DC.) In *The Myth of the Negro Past*, Herskovits convincingly demonstrated that the American Negro was an extension of the African Negro, an African people in the New World,[37] and along the way criticized Frazier's opposite conclusions published in *The Negro Family in the United States* (1939),[38] which were quite similar to those expressed in Herskovits's 1925 essay. The two would exchange searching critiques in 1942 and 1943, and the debate would continue for decades.

This dispute over origins had political as well as cultural implications. As the anthropologist Lee Baker explains, for

Park and Frazier, the belief that American Negroes had no authentic culture corresponded to the viewpoint that problems in contemporary African American communities were, in Frazier's phrase, a case of "incomplete assimilation of western culture."[39] Deprived of any cultural inheritance of their own and barred by discrimination from full entry into white America, Negroes were left, in Frazier's view, with what Baker summarizes as a "pathological culture."[40] The solution, for Frazier and his followers, was to advance social welfare and antidiscrimination policies that would end the Negro's "social isolation" and foster the race's assimilation of normative (white) American practices and values.

By contrast, those who took the Boasian approach saw in the African roots of Negro folk culture further proof of the inherent equality between the races: for them, an essential precondition for ending discrimination was for society to recognize the Negro as the author and inheritor of a valid, authentic culture. While both groups supported antidiscrimination efforts, Boasian anthropology promoted an attitude of cultural relativism, which was at odds with Park and Frazier's emphasis on cultural pathologies. Though disagreements about the best approach to solving inequalities remain ever with us, the intellectual debate over the strength and endurance of Black Americans' African origins was eventually resolved in favor of cultural continuities, including in the fields of music, vocabulary, linguistic structures, speech patterns, and folklore.

That debate arose in part from the curious myth that slave ship captains and/or enslavers on plantations separated their captives from one another by language in an attempt to prevent them from rebelling. This idea peppers sociolinguistic theory and histories of slavery, and it is very much an urban legend today.[41] The historian Herbert Aptheker, in his classic 1943 work *American Negro Slave Revolts*, noted that "language differences were also in this way introduced which tended to make uprisings and plots more difficult."[42] Aptheker footnotes an essay by Park[43] and Frazier's same claim from *The Negro Family in the United States*: "In contrast to the situation in the West Indies, African traditions and practices did not take root and survive in the United States."[44] Frazier also footnotes Park's essay, in which he says, "as soon as they were landed in this country, slaves were immediately divided and shipped in small numbers, frequently no more than one or two at a time, to different plantations. This was the procedure with the very first Negroes brought to this country. It was found easier to deal with the slaves, if they were separated from their kinsmen."[45] Park goes on to say that subsequent generations of American-born enslaved people "had already forgotten or only dimly remembered their life in Africa. . . . Everything that marked [newly arrived slaves from Africa] was regarded as ridiculous and barbaric." Moreover, "the memories of Africa which they brought with them were soon lost."[46] Park's source was an antiabolitionist book published in 1833 by Mrs. A. C. Carmichael,[47] who maintained that "native Africans do not at all like it to be supposed that they retain the customs of their country; and consider themselves wonderfully civilized by their being transplanted from Africa to the West Indies. Creole negroes [those born in the West Indies, not in Africa] invariably consider themselves superior people, and lord it over the native Africans." Park quotes these sentences verbatim as proof of his claim.[48]

And there you have it: the genesis of a false claim, authorized by repetition in footnotes, migrating from sociology to anthropology and on to history, then poured into debates about origins in the fledgling discourse of folklore studies. This argument, based not in fact but rather in the claim of a slavery apologist, would be used as proof that African folktales and African American folktales could not possibly have anything to do with each other. The only problem with these claims is that they are not true. Historically, this sort of ethnic or linguistic separation did not happen, either on slave ship or plantation.[49]

Captured Africans brought their language, their gods, and their culture along with them. They quickly learned to communicate not only on their plantations and other sites of enslavement but also across longer distances. And the telling and retelling of folktales from Africa, as well as those retold from European sources and those invented on the spot, were part of the process of the shaping of an African American culture.

As Jean Toomer put it in an essay he published in 1922, "a [Black middle class] respectability . . . is never so vigorous as when it denounces and rejects the true art of the race's past. They are ashamed of the past made permanent by the spirituals."[50] And because of middle-class attitudes about "respectability" and opinions such as those of Rogers and Schuyler, the Harlem Renaissance must be seen as a road on the path to the creation of a subsequent renaissance in Black writing that would arise in the late sixties, be constructed on a foundation of Black vernacular forms such as blues and jazz, signifying, and other Black vernacular linguistic rituals, and reach maturity in the works of writers such as Toni Morrison and Alice Walker, the pioneers of the Black women's literary movement of the 1970s.

◇

CHAPTER SIX

Modernism and Its Discontents

ZORA NEALE HURSTON AND RICHARD WRIGHT PLAY THE DOZENS

A besotted young Black man, Chris Washington, heads upstate for a meet-the-parents weekend with the love of his life, Rose Armitage. What gradually unfolds is a vivid depiction of the postmodern Black nightmare, which director Jordan Peele has named "The Sunken Garden," in his remarkable film *Get Out*.

What we watch, in horror, is the white brain literally being implanted into the African American body. Through the sorcery of Missy Armitage's diabolical powers, hypnosis, and some in-home neurosurgery, the Black body is forced into housing white consciousness, surely a long-running nightmare coursing like a leitmotif through the texts mentioned in this book. But what was Peele's source?

In 1903, a thirty-five-year-old scholar and budding political activist named William Edward Burghardt Du Bois published *The Souls of Black Folk*. Subtitled *Essays and Sketches*, Du Bois's 265-page book consisted of thirteen essays and one short story, addressing a wide range of topics including the story of the freedmen in Reconstruction; the political ascendancy of Booker T. Washington; the sublimity of spirituals; the death of Du Bois's only son, Burghardt; and a short story about a lynching. Hailed as a classic even by his contemporaries, the book has been republished well over one hundred times since 1903.

Despite its fragmentary structure, the book's disparate parts contribute to a sense of a whole, like movements in a symphony. Each chapter is pointedly "bicultural," prefaced by both an excerpt from a white poet and a bar of what Du Bois calls the Sorrow Songs, the spirituals, "some echo of haunting melody from the only American music which welled up from Black souls in the dark past."[1]

Du Bois's subject was, in no small part, the largely unarticulated beliefs and practices of American Negroes, who were impatient to burst out of the cotton fields and take their rightful place as Americans. As he saw it, African American culture in 1903 was at once vibrant and disjointed, rooted in an almost medieval agrarian past and yet fiercely restive. Born in the chaos of slavery, the culture had begun to generate a richly variegated body of plots, stories, melodies, and rhythms. In *The Souls of Black Folk*, Du Bois peered closely at the culture of his kin and saw the face of Black America. Or, rather, he saw two faces.

"One ever feels his two-ness—an American, a Negro," Du Bois wrote, "two Souls, two thoughts, two unreconciled strivings, two warring ideals in one dark body, whose dogged strength alone keeps it from being torn asunder."[2] He described this condition as "double-consciousness," and his emphasis on a fractured psyche made *The Souls of Black Folk* a harbinger of the modernist movement that would begin to flower a decade or so later in Europe and America. This is the metaphor that is at the heart of the "Sunken Garden" scene in *Get Out*, an astonishingly brilliant, postmodern riff on Du Bois's powerful trope of Black alienation in an anti-Black racist white America.

Scholars including Werner Sollors, Dickson Bruce, and David Levering Lewis have debated the origins of Du Bois's use of the concept of "double-consciousness," but what is clear is that its roots are multiple, which is telling. Du Bois had studied in Berlin during a Hegel revival, and Hegel, famously, had written on the relationship between a master and a bondsman, whereby each defined himself through the recognition of the other. But the concept comes up, too, in Emerson, who wrote in 1842 of the split between our reflective self, which wanders through the realm of ideas, and our active self, which dwells in the here and now. As Emerson wrote, "The worst feature of this double consciousness is that the two lives, of the understanding and of the soul, which we lead, really show very little relation to each other."[3] Even closer to hand was the term's appearance in late-nineteenth-century psychology. The French psychologist Alfred Binet, writing in his 1890 book *On Double Consciousness*, discusses "bipartition" or "the duplication of consciousness": "each of the consciousnesses occupies a more narrow and more limited field than if there existed one single consciousness containing all the ideas of the subject."[4] William James, who was Du Bois's mentor at Harvard, talked about a "second personality" that characterized "the hypnotic trance."[5]

When Du Bois transposed this concept from the realm of the psyche to the social predicament of the American Negro, he shared with the psychologists the notion that double consciousness was essentially an affliction. "This American world," he complained, yields the Negro "no true self-consciousness, but only lets him see himself through the revelation of the other world. It is a peculiar sensation, this double-consciousness, this sense of always looking at one's self through the eyes of others, of measuring one's soul by the tape of a world that looks on in amused contempt, and pity." Sadly, "the double life every

American Negro must live, as a Negro and as an American," leads inevitably to "a painful self-consciousness, an almost morbid sense of personality and a moral hesitancy which is fatal to self-confidence." The result is "a double life, with double thoughts, double duties and double social classes," and worse, "double words and double ideas," which "tempt the mind to pretense or to revolt, to hypocrisy or to radicalism." Accordingly, Du Bois wanted to make the American Negro whole; and he believed that only desegregation and full equality could make this psychic integration possible.[6]

Yet for subsequent generations of writers, what Du Bois cast as a problem was taken to be the defining condition of modernity itself. The diagnosis, you could say, outlasted the disease. Although Du Bois would publish twenty-two books and thousands of essays and reviews, no work of his has done more to shape an African American literary tradition than *The Souls of Black Folk*, and no metaphor in his intricately layered book has proved more enduring than that of double consciousness.

Du Bois yearned to make the American Negro one and lamented that he was two. Today, the ideal of wholeness has largely been retired, and cultural multiplicity is no longer seen as the problem, but as a solution to the confines of identity itself. Double consciousness, once a disorder, is now the cure. Indeed, the only complaint we moderns have is that Du Bois was too cautious in his accounting. He's conjured "two souls, two thoughts, two unreconciled strivings." Two is not enough.

Du Bois's "double-consciousness" has been the governing metaphor in African American literature and culture throughout the twentieth century, just as the metaphor of dualities or binary oppositions dominated the slave narratives. These are called "controlling tropes" or "master narratives" or "scenes of instruction."

We see its first manifestation in James Weldon Johnson's controversial experimental novel, *The Autobiography of an Ex-Colored Man* (1912), in which Johnson literalized Du Bois's metaphor through a character who is simultaneously "Black" and "white," or neither. The metaphor was extended and redefined again in 1923, when the novelist Jean Toomer published *Cane*, to many critics the most sophisticated work of the entire Harlem Renaissance, a book whose theme and form were the alienation and fragmentation of modernity itself, not merely—or primarily—Black modernity. Here, in this experimental, fragmented novel, perhaps for the first time, a condition affecting Black people serves as a trope, a metaphor, for the human condition. The particular is used to express the universal, the hallmark of any great work of art.

The most dramatic representation or revision of Du Bois's metaphor came in Zora Neale Hurston's 1937 novel,

Their Eyes Were Watching God. It was Hurston's definition of double consciousness, in terms of an African American woman's quest for identity and fulfillment, that set off one of the most bitter debates in the history of African American letters, between Zora Neale Hurston and Richard Wright. The debate became very personal, but it was in fact about modes of representation, about modernism and naturalism itself. In reviews of each other's books, sexual politics met literary politics head-on, for the first time so publicly in African American literary history.

In a very angry and suggestive review in *New Masses*, Wright, three years before he published his classic novel of naturalism, *Native Son*, criticizes both Hurston and her novel:

> Miss Hurston can write, but her prose is cloaked in that facile sensuality that has dogged Negro expression since the days of Phillis Wheatley. Her dialogue manages to catch the psychological movements of the Negro folk-mind in their pure simplicity, but that's as far it goes.
>
> Miss Hurston *voluntarily* continues in her novel the tradition which was *forced* upon the Negro in the theater, that is, the minstrel technique that makes the "white folks" laugh. Her characters eat and laugh and cry and work and kill; they swing like a pendulum eternally in that safe and narrow orbit in which America likes to see the Negro live:

between laughter and tears. . . . The sensory sweep
of her novel carries no theme, no message, no
thought.

"In the main," Wright concludes, "her novel is not addressed to the Negro, but to a white audience whose chau-
vinistic tastes she knows how to satisfy," with the word
"satisfy" serving as a veiled reference to Hurston's depiction of her protagonist's sexuality. He then outright ac-
cuses her of titillating her white male readers: "The
romantic Janie, in the highly-charged language of Miss
Hurston, longed to be a pear tree in blossom and have a
'dust-bearing bee sink into the sanctum of a bloom; the
thousand sister-calyxes arch to meet the love embrace.'"
Wright was not satisfied.[7]

Less than a year later, Wright published *Uncle Tom's
Children*, a collection of four interrelated novellas. Now it
was Hurston's turn. "This is a book about hatreds," she
begins her review. "Mr. Wright serves notice by his title
that he speaks of people in revolt, and his stories are so
grim that the Dismal Swamp of race hatred must be where
they live. Not one act of understanding and sympathy
comes to pass in the entire work. . . . [O]ne wonders what
he would have done had he dealt with plots that touched
the broader and more fundamental phases of Negro life
instead of confining himself to the spectacular."

Wright's hero, Big Boy, she continues, in a most mocking manner, "is a stupid, blundering character, but full of pathos. . . . In the third story, the hero gets the white man most Negro men rail against—the white man who possesses a Negro woman. He gets several of them while he is about the business of choosing to die in a hurricane of bullets and fire because his woman has had a white man.

"There is lavish killing here, perhaps enough to satisfy all male Black readers," but not Miss Hurston, nor anyone who loves Black culture from the *inside*, she suggests: "the reader sees the picture of the South that the communists have been passing around of late. A dismal, hopeless section ruled by brutish hatred and nothing else. Mr. Wright's author's solution, is the solution of the PARTY—state responsibility for everything and individual responsibility for nothing, not even feeding one's self. And march!"

And whereas Wright had criticized Hurston's use of dialect, or Black vernacular speech, in her novel as a form of neo-minstrelsy, Hurston turns the tables on Wright by noting: "Since the author himself is a Negro, his dialect is a puzzling thing. One wonders how he arrived at it. Certainly, he does not write by ear unless he is tone deaf." His dialect is a form of "broken speech," not musical or artistic or expressive of the depths of Black culture at all.[8]

Hurston concludes her review by saying that instead of pandering to the political or "the spectacular," as she puts it, she hoped that Wright would someday be able to find a theme worthy of a great novel, a theme rooted firmly and squarely "in Negro life" itself, and not in sensationalist representations of Black-white violence, rape, and lynching in the South. Hurston describes herself, in her author's biographical note, as having written a novel "of life among her own people," whereas, she implies, Wright is obsessed with the seemingly irresistible force of white people, or white racism, in Black people's lives.

In these two reviews, we see a coded exchange, a debate between the literary forms of modernism and naturalism: Hurston used the mode of lyrical modernism to write her novels; Wright used naturalism. And the difference is between what you think of the role of individual will and individual choice, or "agency," versus environmental factors, or "structure," in the shaping of a person's fate.

We can see this clearly if we reflect on the structure of Wright's fiction. Wright published *Native Son* in 1940, three years after Hurston published *Their Eyes Were Watching God*. His was the first Book-of-the-Month Club selection of a Black author's work. It became a runaway bestseller. In the novel, Bigger Thomas (whose name is a rather obvious play on "Nigger") lives a life of despair in a ghetto in Chicago, one determined by large supraforces of race and class. Bigger's life falls apart when he accidentally murders a rich white girl, the daughter of the man for whom he is a chauffeur. Then he murders his own girlfriend, a Black woman named Bessie. After an intense chase, he is captured and of course found guilty and sentenced to death. He dies in the electric chair.

Native Son is a naturalist novel. It is told in the third person through an omniscient narrator who tells us what Bigger is thinking, what Bigger would say if he only had the words and the knowledge to express himself as eloquently as the narrator does. Bigger doesn't *act*, like Janie Crawford in Hurston's novel does; he *reacts*. Bigger is like a pinball in a pinball machine.

Bigger's life and his life choices are determined by the twin social forces of racism and economic exploitation. He has no choice but to live the life of the walking dead, and ultimately to commit murder to assert and define himself. He is an object, not a subject. Someone has to tell his tale for him; he cannot tell it himself. And the only way to change Bigger's life trajectory—that is, to give him subjectivity, to transform him from an object to a subject— would be to destroy completely the racist, capitalist system in which he is confined.

Wright draws upon naturalism to make the risky argument that Black people stuck in the nightmare cycle of the inner cities are not responsible for their tragic lives, their self-destructive behavior, and the destruction that a murderer such as Bigger wreaks upon society. Instead, they are the true victims. Naturalism, in other words, is a mode of literary narration that embraces structure as the ultimate cause of all social ills and pathological behavior.

As Wright puts it:

> To Bigger and his kind white people were not really people; they were a sort of great natural force, like a stormy sky looming overhead, or like a deep swirling river stretching suddenly at one's feet in the dark. As long as he and his black folks did not go beyond certain limits, there was no need to fear that white force. But whether they feared it or not, each and every day of their lives they lived with it; even when words did not sound its name, they acknowledged its reality. As long as they lived here in this prescribed corner of the city, they paid mute tribute to it.[9]

Later in the book, he continues: "He had been so conditioned in a cramped environment that hard words or kicks alone knocked him upright and made him capable of action—action that was futile because the world was too much for him. It was then that he closed his eyes and struck out blindly, hitting what or whom he could, not looking or caring what or who hit back."[10]

The differences between Richard Wright and Zora Neale Hurston help us to understand how literary form implies or reflects political ideology. The list is long:

· Wright focuses on Black/white confrontation, believing that Black confrontation with anti-Black racism is everything. Hurston's work is more about Black-Black interactions in an all-Black world, where white people are offstage.

· Wright writes in the third person. Hurston writes in the first person.

· Wright's protagonist Bigger Thomas is static. Hurston's Janie Crawford is dynamic.

· To Wright, a character's actions are determined by the system, by large supraforces such as racism, capitalism, or economics. Hurston's characters' actions are determined by individual will and individual choices. They make their own fates.

· Finally, for Wright, W. E. B. Du Bois's "double-consciousness" is an *affliction*. It is the state of false consciousness, consciousness reflecting an alienation that can only be overcome through class-based revolution. For Hurston, double consciousness is *healthy*. It is the condition of modernity itself. And it is only when Janie learns that she has double consciousness—an inside and an outside that she must learn to navigate between—that she finds true liberation, reflected in her sexual liberation, in her decision to take as a lover a man much younger than she is, a man whom for the first time she truly loves.

In the previous chapter I quoted Du Bois's essay "Criteria of Negro Art," from 1926, in which he upbraids the writers of the Harlem Renaissance because "[w]e are ashamed of sex and we lower our eyes when people will talk of it. Our religion holds us in superstition. Our worst side has been so shamelessly emphasized that we are denying we have or ever had a worst side. In all sorts of ways we are hemmed in and our new young artists have got to fight their way to freedom." Hurston was among Du Bois's readership, and, implicitly at least, she accepted this challenge that he issued when she published *Their Eyes Were Watching God* some eleven years later, which takes the music of the language of the Black vernacular, including linguistic rituals such as playing the dozens and signifying, and turns them into the language of fiction—into art.

In his review, Wright had criticized Hurston for representing Janie's experiencing her first orgasm under a pear tree, using language he felt was meant to titillate white readers, especially white males. Hurston felt, on the contrary, that it was Wright who was pandering to white readers, especially white males, by writing about Black violence against white racists. But it is clear that Wright was deeply troubled that Hurston created a Black female character who not only has healthy sexual fantasies, but who also goes through two marriages to Black men whom she doesn't love, who abuse her in one way or another, before finding ultimate sexual satisfaction with a younger man who is much darker than she is, a lower-class, uneducated Black man who teaches her how to play checkers, shoot a gun, and work and make love for the sheer pleasure of both.

For Hurston, then, double consciousness—or the recognition that one is made up of many consciousnesses, not just two (a Negro, an American, as Du Bois put it)—is the beginning of freedom, of genuine self-knowledge, of the ultimate liberation, which will inevitably be individual, not based on one's group affiliation or ethnic identity or so-called race. Now that she realizes that she has a double consciousness and can navigate between these two worlds, Janie gains her voice. She speaks herself free by signifying upon, or playing the dozens upon, her second husband Joe's manhood by implying that he is impotent in front of all of his friends, a very cold moment in the history of the Negro.

Reducing a nation within a nation (which as of 2021 was about forty-seven million people), more than half of them female, to one identity, "Black," Hurston argues, is to obscure the sheer complexity of the Black experience, indeed, of the human experience itself. Hurston is asking Black people to decide if their identities are more complicated than the fact of their color. Ralph Ellison, echoing Hurston in his great novel *Invisible Man*, has his protagonist ask: "Until some gang succeeds in putting the world in a strait jacket, its definition is possibility. . . . Whence

all this passion toward conformity anyway?—diversity is
the word. Let man keep his many parts and you'll have no
tyrant states. . . . Our fate is to become one, and yet
many— This is not prophecy, but description."[11]

Hurston would have African Americans ask themselves, Is all of my being, is the complex and marvelous
individual that I am, capable of being boiled down to one
among many of my identities, that fact of race? She would
ask every African American to ask themselves, Is that one
identity, of all your identities, what you want on your
tombstone: Here lies an African American?

Hurston's is the voice of multiplicity, the voice of the
privilege to embrace diversity, within diversity; the voice
for allowing every individual within a minority group, be
it based on ethnicity, religion, or gender, to express their
individuality, their personalities, in whatever idiosyncratic
way they choose. Hurston is also the novelist who finally
understood—just as Langston Hughes and Sterling A.
Brown saw in poetry—that the wellspring of a great tradition in African American fiction could be forged out of
the language of the people, the language of the Black
masses; that it didn't need to be "refined" or "cleaned up"
or "mutated" into classical European forms to be "presentable" to the larger American society; that the art forms
that the sons and daughters of those who lived in bondage
had created were not "an embarrassment to the race"; and,

most important, that artistic expression is, first and last, the province of the artist.

Perhaps this contrast between Wright's vision of Blackness as crafted in *Native Son* and that of Hurston in *Their Eyes Were Watching God* helps us to understand why Hurston's brand of lyrical modernism has blossomed so splendidly and profoundly in the work of Black women writers such as Toni Morrison, Alice Walker, Gayl Jones, and Jamaica Kincaid, while Wright's naturalism seems to have found its voice not in contemporary Black fiction, but rather in the rhetorical strategy of Ta-Nehisi Coates's extended essay *Between the World and Me* (which is the title of a poem written by Wright), and in that stream of hip-hop known as gangsta rap, in language that is direct and polemical, and "in your face" rather than the multilayered, polyvocal language characteristic of great literary art, literary language that signifies on several levels, not just one.

Hurston drew extensively from folklore as well. Sterling Brown hailed Hurston's role in retrieving Negro folklore from those who would denigrate, devalue, or underestimate it: "Miss Hurston is a trained anthropologist, who brings a great zest to both the collecting and the rendering of the 'big old lies' of her native South."[12] In a way, Brown is the link between Hurston and an entire "school" of modernists and postmodernists whose work is constructed, in various ways, on the bedrock of Black folklore and other vernacular forms, especially the way Black people have spoken and continue to speak African American versions of American English. I'm thinking especially of Ralph Ellison and Albert Murray, Alice Walker and Toni Morrison, though the list of superb writers in this branch of the African American tradition is long and distinguished, and would have to include Ishmael Reed, Toni Cade Bambara, Leon Forrest, and a host of other brilliant authors. In other words, an entire branch, or school, of African American literature unfolded from the fiction of Zora Neale Hurston and the poetry of Langston Hughes and Sterling A. Brown, themselves indebted to the literary experimentation with Black vernacular traditions in the work of James Weldon Johnson, especially *God's Trombones*, and its predecessor, Jean Toomer's *Cane*.

In part because of Hurston's efforts to collect Negro folklore, in part because of her experiments with folklore in her novel, both Richard Wright and Ralph Ellison articulated the fundamental importance of Black folklore and vernacular to defining—and *mining*—a genuine "Black aesthetic," a theoretical position that Toni Morrison would also embrace and embody in her fiction.

Writing in 1937 from within a Marxist aesthetic but struggling to reconcile it with a nascent cultural nationalism, Wright had this to say:

Negro folklore contains, in a measure that puts to shame more deliberate forms of Negro expression, the collective sense of Negro life in America. Let those who shy at the nationalist implications of Negro life look at this body of folklore, living and powerful, which rose out of a unified sense of common life and a common fate. Here are those vital beginnings of a recognition of value in life as it is *lived*, a recognition that marks the emergence of a new culture in the shell of the old. And at the moment this process starts, at the moment when a people begin to realize a *meaning* in their suffering, the civilization that engenders that suffering is doomed.[13]

Although Wright didn't manage to draw upon the vibrancy of the folk tradition in his fictions, Ellison did. He refers to the power and importance of Black folklore again and again in his critical writings, nowhere more powerfully than in this statement in 1967:

We have been exiled in our own land and, as for our efforts at writing, we have been little better than silent because we have not been cunning. I find this rather astounding because I feel that Negro American folklore is very powerful, wonderful, and universal. And it became so by expressing a people who were assertive, eclectic, and irreverent before all the oral and written literature that came within its grasp. It took what it needed to express its sense of life and rejected what it could not use. . . . What we have achieved in folklore has seldom been achieved in the novel, the short story, or poetry. In the folklore we tell what Negro experience really is. We back away from the chaos of experience and from ourselves, and we depict the humor as well as the horror of living. We project Negro life in a metaphysical perspective and we have seen it with a complexity of vision that seldom gets into our writing.[14]

And though he would have been most reluctant to admit it, Ellison's debt to Hurston's uses of folklore was a considerable one.

Hurston herself collected folklore, using "the spy-glass of Anthropology," theorized about folklore, and rendered folklore in novels, especially in *Their Eyes Were Watching God*. In her insightful essay "Characteristics of Negro Expression," Hurston writes: "Negro folklore is not a thing of the past. It is still in the making. Its great variety shows the adaptability of the Black man: nothing is too old or too new, domestic or foreign, high or low, for his use. God and the Devil are paired, and are treated no more reverently than Rockefeller and Ford. . . . The automobile is ranged alongside of the oxcart. The angels and the apostles walk and talk like section hands. And through it all walks Jack, the greatest cultural hero of the south; Jack beats them all—even the Devil, who is often smarter than God."[15]

Hurston noted, prophetically, that the folklore invented by African Americans is "still in the making." No one has voiced this idea more powerfully, both in her essays and in her fictions, than Toni Morrison: "We don't live in places where we can hear . . . stories anymore; parents don't sit around and tell their children those classical, mythological archetypal stories that we heard years ago. But new information has got to get out, and there are several ways to do it. One is in the novel. I regard it as a way to accomplish certain very strong functions."[16] Ishmael Reed's work exemplifies a similar aesthetic, different from Morrison's in that his preferred forms are satire and parody, but related just the same. Morrison and Reed, among several other Black writers, constitute the postmodern or—to use a term coined by Nobel Laureate Wole Soyinka—the "mythopoetic" pole in the history of Black representational strategies that descend from Toomer, Hughes, Brown, and Hurston, among others, as opposed to the practice of literary realism or naturalism best exemplified by Wright's classic novel *Native Son* and his literary heirs. Because of the enormous influence of Morrison's novels on other Black writers, the size of her readership, the plethora of critical commentary that her novels have engendered, her several extended reflections on her method of composition amounting, in effect, to her "figure in the carpet," as Henry James put it,[17] her own theory of the nature and function of the African American novel, there can be no question that African American folklore is alive and well as a shaping influence in the African American literary tradition.

Those of us concerned about the political destiny of the African American people, and who love the brilliance and the beauty of the African American tradition, should, of course, be concerned about the images of Black people circulated in literature and art and music. But first and foremost, we have to fight for the freedom of the artist to create their literary worlds unencumbered by those who would censor art for "political reasons," even when we most disagree with the contours or politics of the artistic world that that artist has created and represented. These lessons, finally, comprise the enormous moral and aesthetic significance of Zora Neale Hurston's *Their Eyes Were Watching God*.

CHAPTER SEVEN

Sellouts vs. Race Men

ON THE CONCEPT OF PASSING

For my parents' generation and mine, the film *Imitation of Life*, released in 1934, constituted one of the cardinal moments in the shaping of African American culture, first because it was so beautifully filmed and second because it served as a cautionary tale against "passing for white" and "betraying the race." It's also a tearjerker to end all tearjerkers, and I loved watching that original version late at night with my parents when I was a kid.

We might think of *Imitation of Life* as an urtext of Black cultural consciousness, an extremely popular and deeply moving film seen by so many people that it fundamentally shaped American attitudes for two or three generations about what constitutes a racial "sellout"—someone who "passes" and thus "betrays" her or his Blackness by abandoning the race entirely. Passing is the first cousin of selling out, though you don't have to pass for white, literally, to sell out. You might think of selling out, so-called, as metaphorically passing: selling your soul and the soul of the race for profit. The polar opposite of the "sellout" who passes is a "race man" or a "race woman," a person loyal to Black people, who defends Black people, is proud of being Black himself or herself, and is proud of other Black people; someone who celebrates the achievements of Black people, Black history, and Black culture with pride. Judge Leon Higginbotham used to say that Thurgood Marshall was a race man and his successor on the Supreme Court, Clarence Thomas, was a sellout. As always, judgments such as these are arbitrary.

Imitation of Life stars Claudette Colbert and Louise Beavers. Beavers is the Black cook (Delilah) who invents a boxed pancake formula that makes the white Colbert (Bea) rich. Delilah was based on Aunt Jemima. The two women live in the same home with their daughters for years, the result of an arrangement in which Delilah agreed to serve as a housekeeper to Bea in exchange for room and board for herself and her daughter, Peola, who looks white and has a long-gone white father. Peola decides to check out of the race and pass for white, abandoning her mother and breaking her heart.

The film, released in 1934 and nominated for three

Academy Awards (Best Picture, Best Assistant Director, and Best Sound Recording), was based on the popular novel of the same name, published in 1933 by Fannie Hurst, a white friend of Langston Hughes and Zora Neale Hurston. (A 1959 remake starring Lana Turner and Juanita Moore changed the details and the characters' names, as did another film, *I Passed for White*, released in 1960, but the focus on race was the same, and another generation of viewers was entranced by the film.)

Imitation of Life is essentially an extended riff on James Weldon Johnson's *The Autobiography of an Ex-Colored Man*, published twenty-two years earlier. For the earlier book, no author was credited, as if it were a genuine autobiography published anonymously. But it was a novel, a story that Johnson made up completely, a novel "passing," as it were, for a nonfiction book about a Black man who actually passed for white. It fooled everybody; people wrote to newspapers saying they personally knew the man who was passing.

Johnson's novel was also being riffed on in a painting called *The Drop Sinister: What Shall We Do with It?*, painted by Harry Willson Watrous around 1913. In it, a family of three sits around a table, under a portrait of the Great Emancipator himself, Abraham Lincoln. The man, presumably the father, possibly a minister, reads a newspaper called *The Christian*, and on the mantel behind him are two crosses flanking a decoration reading "And God said, Let us make man in our image after our likeness." The mother, shown in profile, dark-haired with milky white skin and a thin, possibly even upturned nose, pushes back slightly from the table, where a cherubic blond curly-haired girl stands beside her, looking up at her imploringly. No one in the painting is phenotypically Black. What question has been asked, and what is the answer? Who is "Black" and who is "white" in this painting? Who has the dreaded drop?

W. E. B. Du Bois knew. Upon its debut, the painting was a curiosity, and in *The Crisis* he responded definitively to the confusion with which it was greeted at the New York Academy of Design in 1914. "There was a crowd continually around it," he wrote. "A part of the crowd did not understand it. 'What does it mean?' they asked. Another part pretended that they understood it. 'It is miscegenation,' they croaked." In an issue that also included a feature called "Selected Pictures of Seventy-Nine of Our Baby Friends," with photographs sprinkled throughout of Black children of various skin color and hair color and texture, Du Bois was unambiguous in his assessment of the color line and on which side of it this family stood.

The people in this picture are all "colored;" that is to say the ancestors of all of them two or three generations ago numbered among them full-blooded Negroes. These "colored" folk married and brought to the world a little golden-haired child; today they pause for a moment and sit aghast when they think of this child's future.

What is she? A Negro?

No, she is "white."

But *is* she white?

The United States Census says she is a "Negro."

What earthly difference does it make what she is, so long as she grows up a good, true, capable woman? But her chances for doing this are small!

Why?

Because 90,000,000 of her neighbors, good, Christian, noble, civilized people, are going to insult her, seek to ruin her and slam the door of opportunity in her face the moment they discover *"The Drop Sinister."*[1]

Concepts like passing are dependent upon the fiction of the existence of races as discontinuous essences or entities, plus the law of hypodescent, or the one-drop rule, which was established during slavery to ensure that the enslaver's offspring would remain his property, no matter how mixed or light-skinned they were. Curiously, in Brazil, if you can demonstrate that you have one drop of white ancestry, then you can claim to be white, whereas in America, traditionally, one drop of Black ancestry made you Black. Hence "the drop sinister."

Here is the moment that James Weldon Johnson's young protagonist painfully discovers that he is Black, just as Peola discovered, in school. It is a long passage, worth quoting in full.

One day near the end of my second term at school the principal came into our room, and after talking to the teacher, for some reason said, "I wish all of the white scholars to stand for a moment." I rose with the others. The teacher looked at me, and calling my name said, "You sit down for the present, and rise with the others." I did not quite understand her, and questioned, "Ma'm?" She repeated with a softer tone in her voice, "You sit down now, and rise with the others." I sat down dazed. I saw and heard nothing. When the others were asked to rise I did not know it. When school was dismissed I went out in a kind of stupor. A few of the white boys jeered me, saying, "Oh, you're a nigger too." I heard some Black children say, "We knew he was colored." "Shiny" said to them, "Come along, don't tease him," and thereby won my undying gratitude.

I hurried on as fast as I could, and had gone some distance before I perceived that "Red Head" was walking by my side. After a while he said to me, "Le' me carry your books." I gave him my strap without being able to answer. When we got to my gate he said as he handed me my books, "Say, you know my big red agate? I can't shoot with it any more. I'm going to bring it to school for you to-morrow." I took my books and ran into the house. As I passed through the hallway I saw that my mother was busy with one of her customers; I rushed up into my own little room, shut the door, and went quickly to where my looking-glass hung on the wall. For an instant I was afraid to look, but when I did I looked long and earnestly. I had often heard people say to my mother, "What a pretty boy you have." I was accustomed to hear remarks about my beauty; but, now, for the first time, I became conscious of it, and recognized it. I noticed the ivory whiteness of my skin, the beauty of my mouth, the size and liquid darkness of my eyes, and how the long, black lashes that fringed and shaded them produced an effect that was strangely fascinating even to me. I noticed the softness and glossiness of my dark hair that fell in waves over my temples, making my forehead appear whiter than it really was. How long I stood there gazing at my image I do not know. When I came out and reached the head of the stairs, I heard the lady who had been with my mother going out. I ran down-stairs, and rushed to where my mother was sitting with a piece of work in her hands. I buried my head in her lap and blurted out, "Mother, mother, tell me, am I a nigger?" I could not see her face, but I knew the piece of work dropped to the floor, and I felt her hands on my head. I looked up into her face and repeated, "Tell me, mother, am I a nigger?" There were tears in her eyes, and I could see that she was suffering for me. And then it was that I looked at her critically for the first time. I had thought of her in a childish way only as the most beautiful woman in the world; now I looked at her searching for defects. I could see that her skin was almost brown, that her hair was not so soft as mine, and that she did differ in some way from the other ladies who came to the house; yet, even so, I could see that she was very beautiful, more beautiful than any of them. She must have felt that I was examining her, for she hid her face in my hair, and said with difficulty, "No, my darling, you are not a nigger." She went on, "You are as good as anybody; if anyone calls you a nigger don't notice them." But the more she talked the less was I reassured, and I stopped her by asking, "Well, mother, am I white? Are you white?" She answered tremblingly, "No, I am not white, but your father is one of the greatest men in the country. The best blood of the South is in you—" This suddenly opened up in my heart a fresh chasm of misgiving and fear, and I almost fiercely demanded, "Who is my father? Where is he?" She stroked my hair and said, "I'll tell you about him some day." I sobbed, "I want to know now." She answered, "No, not now."

Perhaps it had to be done, but I have never forgiven the woman who did it so cruelly. It may be that she never knew that she gave me a sword-thrust that day in school which was years in healing.[2]

The novel's protagonist becomes one of the early masters of ragtime. Because he is ashamed of his race—opting to pass for white when he sees a lynching—he decides that he would rather be a mediocre composer of European classical music than a genius composer of ragtime. In an embrace of the politics of respectability, he marries a white woman, moves to an upper-middle-class suburb, and raises two kids as white. The book ends with one of the Black tradition's most sophisticated condemnations of passing and selling out:

> Sometimes it seems to me that I have never really been a Negro, that I have been only a privileged spectator of their inner life; at other times I feel that I have been a coward, a deserter, and I am possessed by a strange longing for my mother's people. . . . [There is a] small but gallant band of colored men who are publicly fighting the cause of their race. . . . Beside them I feel small and selfish. I am an ordinarily successful white man who has made a little money. They are men who are making history and a race. I, too, might have taken part in a work so glorious.
>
> My love for my children makes me glad that I am what I am, and keeps me from desiring to be otherwise; and yet, when I sometimes open a little box in which I still keep my fast yellowing manuscripts, the only tangible remnants of a vanished dream, . . . I cannot repress the thought that, after all, I have chosen the lesser part, that I have sold my birthright for a mess of pottage.[3]

Johnson, like Zora Neale Hurston in *Their Eyes Were Watching God*, is literalizing Du Bois's metaphor of double consciousness. He *lives* this twoness, first as a Black man and then as a white man. He is at once Black and white—so neither, yet both.

In *The Autobiography of an Ex-Colored Man* we can see how the metaphor of double consciousness becomes a character in a novel, the protagonist who decides to perform his life as a white man, to pass. Passing is one extreme in a continuum of "race betrayal," which Du Bois defined as "bleach[ing one's] Negro soul in a flood of white Americanism," maintaining a double self, a public "white" self and a private "Black" cultural self, of which one is ashamed: "The history of the American Negro is the history of this strife. . . . This waste of double aims, this seeking to satisfy two unreconciled ideals, has wrought sad havoc with the courage and faith and deeds of ten thousand thousand people,—has sent them often wooing false gods and invoking false means of salvation, and at times has even seemed about to make them ashamed of themselves"—so "ashamed of themselves," in fact, that in "passing," in this sense, they would deny their connections to or affinity for Black culture, or reject their responsibilities to the larger Black community.[4]

Passing could take at least three forms. First, a Black person could literally pass for white, and therefore move out of the race. Second, they could pass by "classing off," as a character in *Their Eyes Were Watching God* puts it— acting as if the Black upper class, or the upper-middle class, were a race apart from lower-class Black people. Du Bois described this in *The Philadelphia Negro* in 1899, and many people in the New Negro movement during the Harlem Renaissance enacted this as well. Third, Black people could sell out by becoming public spokespersons for policies or opinions that seemed to work against the greater good of the race. Historically, take, for example, a Black person who enslaved other Black people or facili- tated their enslavement. More recently, take the case of a Black person who was himself the beneficiary of affirma- tive action college admissions policies and hiring prac- tices, and whose nomination and appointment to the US Supreme Court was clearly rooted in affirmative action, and who voted with the majority of (white) justices to roll back affirmative action. Does he have the right to do that? After all, is not each member of an ethnic group or reli- gious group an individual with the right to their own be- liefs according to their own conscience and convictions? Not according to the long tradition of the race man and the race woman.

How does one "betray" or "sell out" an entire race? Re- call Du Bois's important statement on the subject, in chapter 10 of *The Souls of Black Folk*: "From the double life every American Negro must live, as a Negro and as an American. . . . Such a double life, with double thoughts, double duties, and double social classes, must give rise to double words and double ideals, and tempt the mind to pretence or revolt, to hypocrisy or to radicalism."[5]

Think about this concept: double thoughts, double duties, double words, double ideals, double social classes. These words could be the epigraph to James Weldon Johnson's novel. *The Autobiography of an Ex-Colored Man* is the story of the ultimate sellout, a would-be race man who is phenotypically illegible, who commits what we might think of as racial suicide, just as Peola does in *Imitation of Life*. Racial suicide is erasing one's Blackness, denying one's Black ancestry. In effect, a person who passes is wearing a mask—one form of a complex aspect of Black culture immortalized by the turn-of-the-century Black poet Paul Laurence Dunbar in the poem "We Wear the Mask":

> We wear the mask that grins and lies,
> It hides our cheeks and shades our eyes,—
> This debt we pay to human guile;
> With torn and bleeding hearts we smile,
> And mouth with myriad subtleties.
>
> Why should the world be over-wise,
> In counting all our tears and sighs?

Nay, let them only see us, while
We wear the mask.

We smile, but, O great Christ, our cries
To thee from tortured souls arise.
We sing, but oh the clay is vile
Beneath our feet, and long the mile;
But let the world dream otherwise,
We wear the mask![6]

This concept of wearing a racial "mask" is the key metaphor in E. Franklin Frazier's famous critique of the Black middle class, *Black Bourgeoisie*, published in French in 1956 and in English in 1957. For Frazier, who was writing during the middle of the twentieth century, passing assumed another form, a phenomenon more subtle yet just as pernicious as erasing one's race. And that phenomenon is erasing one's bonds of racial affiliation or fraternal identification with other Black people. The racial mask becomes the social mask, the mask of class, as Frazier puts it in his chapter "Behind the Masks."

Frazier's appraisal of the soullessness of the Black middle class was predicted, again, by Du Bois, in his concept of "Mammonism," or the pursuit of money over values, when he worried about the new Black middle class, as tiny as it was in 1903, "sink[ing] to a question of cash and a lust for gold," as opposed to the pursuit of "the [true] ideals of this people—the strife for another and juster world, the vague dream of righteousness, the mystery of knowing," which he says were once embodied "in the Black World [by] the Preacher and the Teacher."[7]

Frazier's searing assessment of the Black middle class was an extended critique—fifty-four years later—of Du Bois's essay "The Talented Tenth," published in 1903, the same year as *The Souls of Black Folk*. Du Bois did not invent the term; in an April 1896 essay with the same title, Henry Morehouse, the white man for whom Morehouse College was named, wrote, "In the discussion concerning Negro education we should not forget the talented tenth man. An ordinary education may answer for the nine men of mediocrity; but if this is all we offer the talented tenth man, we make a prodigious mistake." Morehouse continues: "The tenth man, with superior natural endowments, symmetrically trained and highly developed, may become a mightier influence, a greater inspiration to others than all the other nine, or nine times nine like them."[8]

By "the Talented Tenth," Du Bois meant what he called "the college-bred Negro." Ten percent of all Black people would have amounted to 890,000 college graduates in 1903, when *Souls* was published. But the actual percentage of "college-bred Negroes" in that year was far less—only 0.034 percent! (For reference, the percentage of African

Americans age twenty-five and over with a four-year de-gree in 1990 was 11.4 percent, and in 2020 it was 26.1 percent.)[9]

Du Bois defined the Talented Tenth as "a saving rem-nant," an "aristocracy of talent and character." "The Negro race," he said, "like all races, is going to be saved by its exceptional men." This exceptionalism, this Talented Tenth, would be built on a foundation of a liberal arts education rather than vocational training, a critique of Booker T. Washington's position. Education would lift up these exceptional men, who would then "[rise and pull] all that are worth the saving up to their vantage ground. This is the history of human progress."[10]

The function of the college-bred Negro, to Du Bois, involves his particular definition of "service." In fact, Du Bois says: "He is, as he ought to be, the group leader, the man who sets the ideals of the community where he lives, directs its thoughts and heads its social movements. It need hardly be argued that the Negro people need social leadership more than most groups; that they have no tra-ditions to fall back upon, no long established customs, no strong family ties, no well defined social classes. All these things must be slowly and painfully evolved."[11]

In conclusion, Du Bois writes: "The Talented Tenth of the Negro race must be made leaders of thought and mis-sionaries of culture among their people. No others can do this work and Negro colleges must train men for it. The Negro race," he repeats, "like all other races, is going to be saved by its exceptional men."[12]

There was no mistaking the elitism in Du Bois's formulation of the Talented Tenth. His identification of this august group came under fire by many, and he himself acknowledged forty-five years later that he had not foreseen the ways in which self-interest rather than sacrifice might drive those who were "prepared" to lead by their education and class position. In his own self-critique, in 1948, he wrote:

> I assumed that with knowledge, sacrifice would automatically follow. In my youth and idealism, I did not realize that selfishness is even more natural than sacrifice. . . . When I came out of college and into the world of work, I realized that it was quite possible that my plan of training a talented tenth might put in control and power, a group of selfish, self-indulgent, well-to-do men, whose basic interest in solving the Negro problem was personal; personal freedom and unhampered enjoyment and use of the world, without any real care, or certainly no arousing care, as to what became of the mass of American Negroes, or of the mass of any people. My Talented Tenth, I could see, might result in a sort of interracial free for all, with the devil taking the hindmost and the foremost taking anything they could lay hands on.

This, historically, has always been the danger of aristocracy.[13]

The end result of this "saving" of the race by the Talented Tenth was not "pride in a cultural group," as he had wished and anticipated. Rather, he writes, "they wanted to be Americans, and they did not care so much what kind of folk Americans were, as for the right to be one of them." Du Bois believed that many of the members of this group wanted "the Negro" to disappear, both racially and culturally. Taken to its logical extreme, the end of segregation would mean the end of "the Negro."[14]

Du Bois, of course, was not willing to let go of Black culture and through the first half of the century had come to see Black culture more broadly. In 1948 he urged the creation of a New Talented Tenth, a socially responsible, socially conscious leadership class that would become the "vanguard" for political reform, beacons of democracy and social equality not only in the United States but also in alliance with third-world, especially African, anticolonial movements, throughout what Du Bois elsewhere calls the "worlds of color."

Back in the United States, we do see much work at this time being done to dismantle segregation, if not to disappear Negro life entirely, certainly to disappear the limitations on life choices that being "a Negro" represented.

Brown v. Board of Education, most famously, successfully argued that "separate" was inherently unequal. But think about all-Black churches, historically Black colleges and universities, Black sororities and fraternities, Black social and cultural institutions, Black holidays, and Black cultural festivals. Does their separateness make them unequal or, by implication, lesser? Would we want to lose those, too, even as we wish for the end of the subpar institutions created by segregation? Absolutely not. Still, for many Black people at the time, integration was the sign of total success: assimilation into American culture meant shaking off the "taint" of being "the Negro"—"a social problem," as Du Bois once put it.

It was this environment that gave rise to E. Franklin Frazier's controversial critique of his titular "Black bourgeoisie." Frazier, as I mentioned, initially published his book in French, just four years after Frantz Fanon, in Paris, published *Black Skin, White Masks*, in which he explores the psychological effects of colonization on the Black middle class throughout Africa and the Caribbean. In many ways, Frazier's book is riffing on Fanon's powerful study.

Frazier's argument had five salient points:

First, the Black middle class is characterized by self-hatred, and that self-hatred leads it to scorn lower-class Black people: "Since the black bourgeoisie live largely in a world of make-believe, the masks which they wear to play their sorry roles conceal the feelings of inferiority and of insecurity and the frustrations that haunt their inner lives. Despite their attempt to escape from real identification with the masses of Negroes, they cannot escape the mark of oppression any more than their less favored kinsmen. In attempting to escape identification with the black masses, they have developed a self-hatred that reveals itself in their deprecation of the physical and social characteristics of Negroes."[15]

Second, deep down, Frazier argues, most members of the Black middle class secretly harbor a desire to be white, "since [expressing it] would be an admission of their feeling of inferiority." Instead, "the black bourgeoisie constantly boast of their pride in their identification as Negroes. But when one studies the attitude of this class in regard to the physical traits or the social characteristics of Negroes, it becomes clear that the black bourgeoisie do not really wish to be identified with Negroes."[16]

Third, Frazier ties what he sees as Black "self-hatred and guilt feelings" (which he calls "repressed hostilities") to three things: the surprising amount of antisemitism within the Black community; the rejection of an identification with African culture; and persistent claims of a mythical Native American ancestor on so many Black family trees. He writes:

Because middle-class Negroes are unable to in-
dulge in aggressions against whites as such, they
will sometimes make other minority groups the
object of their hostilities. . . . They blame the Jew
for the poverty of Negroes and for their own fail-
ures and inefficiencies in their business undertak-
ings. In expressing their hostilities towards Jews,
they are attempting at the same time to identify
with the white American majority.

The repressed hostilities of middle-class Negroes to whites are not only directed towards other
minority groups but inward toward themselves.
This results in self-hatred. . . . While pretending
to be proud of being a Negro, they ridicule Negroid physical characteristics and seek to modify
or efface them as much as possible. Within their
own groups they constantly proclaim that "niggers"
make them sick. . . . They are insulted if they are
identified with Africans. They refuse to join orga-
nizations that are interested in Africa. If they are
of mixed ancestry, they may boast of the fact that
they have Indian ancestry.[17]

Fourth, given all these things, Frazier argues, the
Black middle class seeks to escape this psychological
plight and "their feelings of inferiority" through delusions
involving conspicuous consumption, "enhanced by the belief that wealth will gain them acceptance in American
life. . . . [M]iddle-class Negroes make a fetish of material
things or physical possessions."[18]

Finally, and perhaps most relevant to us, Frazier argues that it is "this self-hatred of middle-class Negroes" that explains Booker T. Washington's famous saying that Black people were like "crabs in a barrel," pulling each other down whenever one tries to escape: It "is often revealed in the keen competition which exists among them for status and recognition. This keen competition is the result of the frustrations which they experience in attempting to obtain acceptance and recognition by whites. Middle-class Negroes are constantly criticizing and belittling Negroes who achieve some recognition or who acquire a status above them. They prefer to submit to the authority of whites than to be subordinate to other Negroes. . . . In fact," he concludes, "it is difficult for middle-class Negroes to co-operate in any field of endeavor."[19]

Frazier's critique was written in the mid-fifties, just as the civil rights movement was getting underway, shortly after *Brown v. Board of Education*. When Du Bois heard the news that the Supreme Court had unanimously reversed *Plessy v. Ferguson*, he famously is reported to have said, "I have seen the impossible happen."[20] Frazier would live to see the impossible as well, in some part precisely because of the power of his critique, which stung the Black middle class—and especially their children, being educated in the politically militant sixties and seventies—quite severely.

Brown v. Board, which was the culmination of several court cases designed by Charles Hamilton Houston and the NAACP Legal Defense Fund to dismantle de jure segregation, both reflected and reinvigorated a nascent civil rights movement, moving it from the courts to buses, lunch counters, restaurants, and hotels throughout the Dixiecrat, segregated South. The movement's leadership included many people from the very class that Frazier excoriated in his book. Again, this widespread movement doesn't seem to mesh with Frazier's critique.

On the one hand, we can acknowledge that Frazier could not see the possibility of the Black middle class emerging as civil rights warriors when he was writing his book in the mid-fifties—and we can take him to task for this huge blind spot. On the other hand, we have to recognize that Frazier's critique—as strident and hyperbolic as it was—amounted to a call to arms, a bold and direct challenge to the racial loyalty and sense of social responsibility of the Talented Tenth to confront white racism squarely and boldly, but also to fight the devastatingly oppressive effects that centuries of slavery and anti-Black racism had had on what we might think of as the Black psyche. It can in fact be considered one of the catalysts in the development of the civil rights revolution that reached its zenith on August 28, 1963, in the March on Washington.

Even Martin Luther King, Jr., echoed Frazier's critique of the Black bourgeoisie in his remarks at the funeral of the four little girls who were killed less than three weeks later in the September 15, 1963, bombing of the Sixteenth Street Baptist Church in Birmingham, Alabama. King used the occasion to accuse complacent Black people who refused to march of being partly responsible for the deaths of those children. The martyred children, he said, "have something to say to every minister of the gospel who has remained silent behind the safe security of stained-glass windows. . . . They have something to say to every Negro who has passively accepted the evil system of segregation and who has stood on the sidelines in a mighty struggle for justice."[21]

Moreover, the rhetoric of the Black Power movement and the Black Panther Party, epitomized by the anti–Black bourgeoisie Black nationalist politics of Malcolm X, Stokely Carmichael, Eldridge Cleaver, and H. Rap Brown, drew upon Frazier's language and conclusions to challenge the Black middle class to become more militant—to become "Blacker," as it were. We see the fruits of this powerful Black movement in the determination of the new Black middle class—itself created by affirmative action—to succeed in this society without abandoning the Black church, Black art and music, and other traditions created and cherished by their Black ancestors; to succeed in this society without "becoming raceless," without bleaching out their complex cultural and ethnic heritage.

I can attest that when I was a student in the late sixties, Frazier's work was required reading and provided the model of Those Negroes Whom We Most Certainly Did *NOT* Wish to Resemble. But one overarching theme of history is that there are very few political positions that remain, through shifts in historical context, at the same point on the scale of ideology. It's important to remember that today's radical position can be tomorrow's conservative position. Du Bois himself—whom we would never think of as selling out—over the course of his ninety-five-year-long life left the NAACP twice, first resigning under intense pressure in 1934 for defending voluntary segregation among African Americans, and then being fired in 1948 for his left-leaning beliefs.[22] He was also, at various times, an integrationist, a separatist, a Pan-Africanist, a socialist, and a capitalist. He ultimately died in Ghana as an expatriate member of the American Communist Party, ironically on August 27, 1963, on the eve of the March on Washington for Jobs and Freedom, to that date the largest civil rights demonstration in US history.

Perhaps we can pinpoint the long-in-coming culmination of this profound transformation of attitude, starting in the struggle for civil rights in the late 1950s that continued on through the 1960s, to November 4, 2008, when about 95 percent of all Black voters put aside their class differences and cast their votes to make Barack Obama this country's first Black president. But the unmistakable irony—and a very sad one—of the great triumph for racial solidarity and racial consciousness represented by the Black community's overwhelming support for him is that President Obama's victory led almost immediately to proclamations from the right that the legacies of racism no longer existed and that we had overnight entered a mysterious new world that was both "post-Black" and "postracial," which some commentators defined as simply new forms of the longing within American society that we should all pass for white.

What conclusions can we draw about both passing and the concept that one's actions or beliefs can "betray one's race"? What does "race" mean, anyway, when we now know through the latest DNA evidence that virtually all Black Americans have a substantial amount of white ancestry?

Passing was a complex phenomenon. After all, if no one could tell if a person contained that proverbial "drop

sinister," then passing can be seen as something of a revolutionary act, a critique of the definitions of "race" that
Kant invented in 1775. In that sense, passing was a declaration that "race," supposedly fixed by God or nature as an
immutable essence, was really just a social construct, a fiction invented to control and exploit the labor of human
beings of color. In other words, "race" wasn't an essence at
all if the presence of Blackness couldn't actually be de-
tected.

And what about the concept of "race betrayal"? Isn't
that something of a fiction, too, used to control individuality within a group? After all, who is to decide what the
"proper" or the "authentically Black" way of thinking or
behaving actually is? Are we to suppress our individuality
in the name of an imaginary Board of Black Censorship?
Are we to conform to the dictates of public opinion, even
Black public opinion, if we morally or ethically disagree
with it? To quote the groundbreaking cultural critic Stuart Hall:

> . . . I simply want to remind you that the model
> being proposed here is closer to that of how a lan-
> guage works than of how our biology is or our
> physiologies work. That race is more like a lan-
> guage, than it is like the way in which we are bio-
> logically constituted. You may think that's an
> absurd and ridiculous thing to say; you may even

now be surreptitiously glancing around the room, just to make sure that you know your visual appearances are in full working order. I assure you they are: people do look rather peculiar, some of them are brown, some of them are quite black, some of you are pretty brown, some of you are really disgustingly pink in the current light. But, there's nothing wrong with your appearances, but I want to insist to you that nevertheless, the argument that I want to make to you is that *race works like a language*. And signifiers refer to the systems and concepts of the classification of a culture to its practices for *making meaning*. And those things gain their meaning, not because of what they contain in their essence, but in the shifting relations of difference, which they establish with other concepts and ideas in a signifying field. Their meaning, because it is relational, and not essential, can never be finally fixed, but is subject to the constant process of redefinition and appropriation: to the losing of old meanings, and appropriation and collection and contracting of new ones, to the endless process of being constantly resignified, made to mean something different in different cultures, in different historical formations at different moments of time.[23]

Here's what I have to say about the very concept of "race betrayal." You can like ice hockey, country music, yodeling, cross-country skiing, cucumber sandwiches, and wearing kilts, and still be as culturally "Black" as the most militant Black nationalist. If there are forty-seven million Black people in America, that means there are forty-seven million ways "legitimately" to be Black. As I have tried to indicate in this book, my list of the especially heroic people in the history of the race is composed of those brave individuals who never, ever let anybody tell them how to be Black. And it is my fondest hope that my granddaughter, Ellie, will be added to that list.

Policing the Color Line

The freedom to write has a special resonance for Black authors, because for so many of them, that freedom was hard-won. "Liberation" and "literacy" were inextricable. "For the horrors of the American Negro's life there has been almost no language," as James Baldwin once noted.[1] Recall, first, that in many states it was illegal for an enslaved person even to learn how to read or write. Then the barbarities of the slave trade, the Middle Passage, and cradle-to-grave bondage were followed by another century of lynching, Jim Crow segregation, disenfranchisement, and officially sanctioned forms of violence. Does the English language fail us, Baldwin wonders, in the face of racist terror? No, he decides; we must embrace it, occupy it, refashion it in our images, speak it in our own voices. We must deploy it to redress this terror. "To accept one's past—one's history," Baldwin insisted, "is not the same as drowning with it; it is learning how to use it." This, surely, is integral to the freedom to write—the freedom to bear witness to the full range of our common humanity, and all that that entails, no matter how uncomfortable the process can be.

And what of the freedom to learn? Who has the right to study, the right to teach, to broach fraught subjects? These questions take on a new urgency now when partisans in various states are passing laws and resolutions that regulate what teachers can discuss in their classrooms, aiming to exclude critical race theory, *The New York Times*'s 1619 Project, and even words such as "multiculturalism," "equity," and "whiteness." Consider Ron DeSantis, the governor of Florida as of this writing, and an aspirant to higher office, who has objected to a proposed high school course in African American studies. Lurking behind his concerns is a long and complex series of debates about the role of slavery and race in American schools.[2]

"We believe in teaching kids facts and how to think, but we don't believe they should have an agenda imposed on them," Governor DeSantis said. He also decried what he called "indoctrination."[3]

School is one of the first places where society begins to shape our sense of what it means to be an American. It is in our schools that we learn how to become citizens, that we encounter the first civics lessons that either reinforce or counter the myths and fables we have gleaned at home. Each day of first grade in my elementary school in Piedmont, West Virginia, in 1956 began with the Pledge of Allegiance to the flag, followed by "America (My Country, 'Tis of Thee)." To this day, I cannot prevent my right hand from darting to my heart at the words of either.

It is through such rituals, repeated over and over, that certain "truths" become second nature, "self-evident," as it were. This is how the foundations of our understanding of our great nation's history are laid.

Even if we give the governor the benefit of the doubt as to why he has denounced the original version of the College Board's AP curriculum in African American studies, his intervention nevertheless follows in a long tradition of bitter, politically suspect battles over the interpretation of three seminal periods in the history of American racial relations: the Civil War; the twelve years following the war, known as Reconstruction; and Reconstruction's brutal rollback. This last period, characterized by its adherents as the "Redemption" of the former Confederacy, saw the imposition of Jim Crow segregation, the reimposition of white supremacy, and the justification of both through a masterfully executed propaganda effort.

This so-called Lost Cause movement was, in effect, a

take-no-prisoners social media war in which politicians and amateur historians joined forces to police the historical profession. And no single group or person was more pivotal to "the dissemination of the truths of Confederate history, earnestly and fully and officially," than the historian general of the United Daughters of the Confederacy, Mildred Lewis Rutherford, of Athens, Georgia.[4] Rutherford was a descendant of a long line of enslavers; her maternal grandfather owned Black people as early as 1820, and her maternal uncle, Howell Cobb, secretary of the treasury under President James Buchanan, owned some two hundred men, women, and children in 1840. Rutherford served as the principal of the Lucy Cobb Institute (a school for girls in Athens) and vice president of the Stone Mountain Memorial project, the former Confederacy's version of Mount Rushmore.[5]

As the historian David Blight notes, "Rutherford gave new meaning to the term 'die-hard.'" Indeed, she "considered the Confederacy 'acquitted as blameless' at the bar of history, and sought its vindication with a political fervor that would rival the ministry of propaganda in any twentieth-century dictatorship."[6] And she felt that the crimes of Reconstruction "made the Ku Klux Klan a necessity."[7] As I pointed out in a PBS documentary on the rise and fall of Reconstruction, Rutherford intuitively understood the direct connection between history lessons taught in the classroom and the Lost Cause racial order being imposed outside it, and she sought to cement that relationship with zeal and efficacy. She understood that what is inscribed on the blackboard translates directly to social practices unfolding on the street.

"Realizing that the textbooks in history and literature which the children of the South are now studying, and even the ones from which many of their parents studied before them," she wrote, in *A Measuring Rod to Test Text Books, and Reference Books in Schools, Colleges and Libraries*, "are in many respects unjust to the South and her institutions, and that a far greater injustice and danger is threatening the South today from the late histories which are being published, guilty not only of misrepresentations but of gross omissions, refusing to give the South credit for what she has accomplished . . . I have prepared, as it were, a testing or measuring rod."[8] And Rutherford used that measuring rod to wage a systematic campaign to redefine the Civil War not as our nation's war to end the evils of slavery but as "the War Between the States," because, as she wrote elsewhere, "the negroes of the South were never called slaves." And they were "well fed, well clothed and well housed."[9]

Of the more than twenty-five books and pamphlets that Rutherford published, none was more important than *A Measuring Rod*. Published in 1920, her user-friendly pamphlet was meant to be the index "by which every text-book on history and literature in Southern schools should be tested by those desiring the truth." The pamphlet was designed to make it easy for "all authorities charged with the selection of textbooks for colleges, schools and all scholastic institutions to measure all books offered for adoption by this 'Measuring Rod,' and adopt none which do not accord full justice to the South." What's more, her campaign was retroactive. As the historian Donald Yaco-vone tells us in his recent book *Teaching White Supremacy*, Rutherford insisted that librarians "should scrawl 'unjust to the South' on the title pages" of any "unacceptable" books "already in their collections."[10]

On a page headed ominously by the word "Warning," Rutherford provides a handy list of what a teacher or a librarian should "reject" or "not reject."

> Reject a book that speaks of the Constitution other than a Compact between Sovereign States.

> Reject a text-book that does not give the principles for which the South fought in 1861, and does not clearly outline the interferences with the rights guaranteed to the South by the Constitution, and which caused secession.

> Reject a book that calls the Confederate soldier a traitor or rebel, and the war a rebellion.

Reject a book that says the South fought to hold her slaves.

Reject a book that speaks of the slaveholder of the South as cruel and unjust to his slaves.

And my absolute favorite:

Reject a text-book that glorifies Abraham Lincoln and villifies [*sic*] Jefferson Davis, unless a truthful cause can be found for such glorification and vil-lification [*sic*] before 1865.

And how were such textbooks to account for slavery? "This was an education that taught the negro self-control, obedience and perseverance—yes, taught him to realize his weaknesses and how to grow stronger for the battle of life," Rutherford wrote in 1923 in *The South Must Have Her Rightful Place in History.* "The institution of slavery as it was in the South, far from degrading the negro, was fast elevating him above his nature and his race."[11] For Rutherford, who lectured dressed in antebellum hoop gowns, the war over how to interpret the recent past was all about establishing the racial order of the present: "The truth must be told, and you must read it, and be ready to answer it." Unless this is done, "in a few years there will be no South about which to write the history."[12]

In other words, Rutherford's common core was the Lost Cause. And it will come as no surprise that this written propaganda effort was accompanied by the construction of many of the Confederate monuments that have dotted the southern landscape since.

While it's safe to assume that most contemporary historians of the Civil War and Reconstruction are of similar minds about Rutherford and the Lost Cause, it's also true that one of the most fascinating aspects of African American studies is the rich history of debate over issues like this, and especially over what it has meant—and continues to mean—to be "Black" in a nation where human slavery constituted the core of the economic system for two and a half centuries.

Heated debates within the Black community, beginning as early as the first decades of the nineteenth century, have ranged from what names "the race" should publicly call itself (William Whipper versus James McCune Smith) to whether or not enslaved men and women should rise in arms against their masters (Henry Highland Garnet versus Frederick Douglass). Ought we to pursue economic development or political rights (Booker T. Washington versus W. E. B. Du Bois)? Should Black people return to Africa (Marcus Garvey versus W. E. B. Du Bois)? Should we admit publicly the pivotal role of

African elites in enslaving our ancestors (Ali Mazrui versus Wole Soyinka)?

Add to these questions ongoing arguments over sexism, socialism and capitalism, reparations, antisemitism, and homophobia and transphobia. It is often surprising to students to learn that there has never been one way to "be Black" among Black Americans, nor have Black politicians, activists, and scholars ever spoken with one voice or embraced one ideological or theoretical framework. Black America, that "nation in a nation," as the Black abolitionist Martin R. Delany put it, has always been as varied and diverse as the complexions of the people who have identified, or been identified, as its members.

This legacy of debate, fundamental to a fuller understanding of Black history, continues through to recent controversies over academic subjects like Kimberlé Crenshaw's stunningly original and deeply insightful theory of "intersectionality," reparations, Black antisemitism, critical race theory, and the 1619 Project—several of which made Governor DeSantis's hit list.

Why shouldn't students be introduced to these debates? Any good class in Black studies seeks to explore the range of thought on race and racism that Black and white thinkers alike have contributed during our ancestors' fight for their rights in this country. In fact, in my experience, teaching our field through these debates is a rich and nuanced pedagogical strategy, affording students ways to create empathy across differences of opinion, to understand diversity within difference, and to reflect on complex topics from more than one angle. It forces them to critique stereotypes and canards about who we are as a people and what it means to be "authentically" Black. I am not sure which of these ideas has landed one of my own essays on the list of texts the state of Florida found objectionable, but there it is.

The Harvard-trained historian Carter G. Woodson, who in 1926 invented what has become Black History Month, was keenly aware of the role of politics in the classroom, especially Lost Cause interventions. "Starting after the Civil War," he wrote, "the opponents of freedom and social justice decided to work out a program which would enslave the Negroes' mind inasmuch as the freedom of the body has to be conceded.

"It was well understood," Woodson continued, "that if by the teaching of history the white man could be further assured of his superiority and the Negro could be made to feel that he had always been a failure and that the subjection of his will to some other race is necessary the freedman, then, would still be a slave.

"If you can control a man's thinking," Woodson concluded, "you do not have to worry about his action."[13]

Is it fair to see Governor DeSantis's attempts to police the contents of the AP curriculum as just a contemporary version of Mildred Rutherford's Lost Cause textbook campaign? No. But the governor would do well to consider the company that he is keeping. And let's just say that he, no expert in African American history, seems to be gleefully embarked on an effort to censor scholarship about the complexities of the Black past with a determination reminiscent of Rutherford's. While not embracing her cause, DeSantis is complicitous in perpetuating her agenda.

As the Reverend Dr. Martin Luther King, Jr., so aptly put it, "No society can fully repress an ugly past when the ravages persist into the present."[14] Addressing these "ravages," and finding solutions to them—a process that can and should begin in the classroom—can only proceed with open discussions across the ideological spectrum.

Throughout Black history, there has been a long, sad, and often nasty tradition of attempts to censor popular art forms, from the characterization of the blues, ragtime, and jazz as "the devil's music" by guardians of "the politics of respectability" to C. Delores Tucker's campaign to ban gangsta rap music in the 1990s. Hip-hop has been an equal opportunity offender for potential censors: Mark Wichner, the deputy sheriff of Florida's Broward County, brought 2 Live Crew up on obscenity charges in 1990. But there is a crucial difference between Tucker, best known as a civil rights activist, and Wichner, an administrator of justice on behalf of the state, a difference similar to that between Rutherford and DeSantis.

While the urge to censor art—a symbolic form of vigilante policing—is color-blind, there is no equivalence between actual governmental censorship and the would-be censorship of moral crusaders. Many states are following Florida's lead in seeking to bar discussions of race and history in classrooms. The distinction between Mildred Lewis Rutherford and Governor DeSantis? The institutional power differential.

Rutherford wished for the power to summon the state apparatus to circumscribe the narrative of race and racism in our country. DeSantis has that power and has demonstrated his willingness to use it. And it is against this misguided use of state power that those of us who cherish the freedom of inquiry at the heart of our country's educational ideal must take a stand.

But we must not exempt ourselves from scrutiny; whenever we treat an identity as something to be fenced off from people of another identity, we sell short the human imagination. The idea that you have to look a certain way in order to master a certain subject was a prejudice that our forebears—women seeking to write about men, Black people seeking to write about white people—

challenged and overcame. In the same year that Rosa Parks refused to move from the white section of that public bus, Toni Morrison completed a master's thesis at Cornell University on Virginia Woolf and William Faulkner, herself taking a seat in the white section of the modernist canon. Any teacher, any student, any reader, any writer, sufficiently attentive and motivated, must be able to engage freely with whatever subjects they choose. That is not only the essence of education; it's the essence of being human.

The great Wole Soyinka helped me grasp this when I came to study with him at the University of Cambridge almost five decades ago. Despite the fact that I wasn't African, let alone Yoruba, Wole welcomed me into his mythical, metaphysical world, dense with the metaphor, potency, and portent of a set of divinities alien to me. And what exhilaration I felt, exploring these new realms. I was put in mind of a passage from the Book of Jeremiah, drawn from my churchgoing youth in West Virginia: "Call unto me, and I will answer thee, and show thee great and mighty things, which thou knowest not."

But then Black Africa's first Nobel Laureate in literature had himself studied Shakespeare with the great English critic G. Wilson Knight, who later hailed him as one of his most remarkable students. The literary imagination summons us all to dwell above what W. E. B. Du Bois called "the veil" of the color line. As he wrote, yearningly: "I summon Aristotle and Aurelius and what soul I will, and they come all graciously with no scorn or condescension. So, wed with Truth, I dwell above the veil."[15] Du Bois never let anyone tell him to stay in his lane. When he needed to, he paved his own. As a lifelong dissident, he also knew that liberation was not secured by filtering out dissident voices; courage, not comfort, was his ideal.

Essentialism about human identity, including racial identity, is terribly limiting, no matter the context. It denies us the capacity to grow, and to be surprised—and wisdom is precisely the capacity to be surprised. If we declare the very process of forming our identities to be off limits from contestation and debate, we are fundamentally undermining the ideal of public discourse upon which American life is premised. The great feminist scholar and activist Catharine MacKinnon once insisted on "the rather obvious reality that groups are made up of individuals," each with a unique lived reality.[16]

We must be particularly wary of individuals who take it upon themselves to police what can and cannot be said. Hate speech has a long and painful history in our country, but we must take care that the cure not be worse than the disease. Since the earliest years of our republic, Black thinkers have fought racism through language, not against it. Critical race theory, for example, is a field that has done much valuable work in our legal system, serving to counter many all too obvious ways in which so-called color-blind policies have failed Black Americans. But the idea of standpoint epistemology, the idea that only a member of a given group can truly understand that group, not only tries to draw a bright line in an aspect of life that is necessarily ambiguous and complicated, but also further fuels the forces of division. When it comes to free speech, to suggest, as prominent critical race theorists long have, that equality must precede liberty, is simply to do away with the latter without ever securing the former.

And this way of thinking can make it more difficult for us to imagine the just society we so desperately need to bring about. We can neither secure our freedoms nor right the systemic inequities that persist in this country by punishing individuals for their rude remarks. An analysis of racism requires not that we adhere to totalizing doctrines but rather that we emulate scholar-investigators like Douglas Massey, William Julius Wilson, or Gary Orfield: people who, whatever their disagreements, attempt to find out how things work in the real world, never confusing the empirical with the merely anecdotal.

I cannot put it better than the scholar Charles Lawrence, who writes: "I fear that by framing the debate as we have—as one in which the liberty of free speech is in conflict with the elimination of racism—we have advanced the cause of racial oppression and placed the bigot on the moral high ground, fanning the rising flames of racism."[17] Though he does not intend it as such, I read this as a harsh rebuke to the forces that oppose free speech, on both sides. The impulse to police language for its potential offensiveness, or to dictate what areas of intellectual inquiry or creative expression are available to whom, does harm to the very cause it means to bolster: indeed, the ability to take an interest in the diversity of experience, to imagine the different ways one might live in the world, is the basis of human empathy.

What we owe to each other, and to ourselves, is a shared sense of wonder and awe as we contemplate works of the human imagination across space and time, works created by people who don't look like us and who, in so many cases, would be astonished that we know their work and their names. Social identities can connect us in multiple and overlapping ways; they are not protected but betrayed when we turn them into silos with sentries. The freedom to write can thrive only if we protect the freedom to read—and to learn. And perhaps the first thing to learn, in these storm-battered times, is that we could all do with more humility, and more humanity.

Acknowledgments

◇

The seven chapters in this book are essays that I revised from the lectures that I delivered in Harvard's Introduction to African American Studies class, which I have had the pleasure of co-teaching with colleagues in the Department of African and African American Studies for many years. After each lecture, I would revise the text in response to comments from our students and from my own sense of aspects of my arguments that could be made clearer and stronger. Every professor understands that lectures are dynamic, not static, and part of the power of a lecture depends on who is listening. I thank my students for questioning and challenging me each year, and I hope the lessons I've sought to impart stay with them long after they leave the hallowed halls of Harvard. Great thanks also go to my co-teachers Evelyn Brooks Higginbotham, with whom I conceived the course from which these lectures arose; Lawrence Douglas Bobo; and Evelynn

Hammonds. The book's final essay was a response that I published in *The New York Times* to attempts by Governor Ron DeSantis to censor the African American Studies AP curriculum in the state of Florida.

For their brilliant research and editorial skills, I would like to thank Kevin Burke, Rob Heinrich, and Julie Wolf. I would also like to thank my editors at Penguin, Scott Moyers and Helen Rouner; my literary agents, David Kuhn, Nate Muscato, and Helen Hicks; my former literary agents, Lynn Nesbit, Tina Bennett, and Paul Lucas; my literary lawyer, Bennett Ashley; Ari Emanuel, Bradley Singer, and Vanessa Hulley at WME; my editor at *The New York Times*, Aaron Retica; Casper Grathwohl and Damon Zucca at Oxford University Press; Marian Johnson, Julia Reidhead, and Carol Bemis at W. W. Norton; and Robert Weil at Liveright. At the Hutchins Center, I thank executive director Abby Wolf, associate director Shawn Lee, Velma DuPont, and Sandra Mancebo. Special thanks go to Amy Gosdanian, who is the anchor in the storm and a never-failing source of the most generous moral support, unflappable good cheer, and astonishingly brilliant organizational wizardry. I would also like to thank several colleagues and friends, each of whom inspired or encouraged my work in various ways, including the following: Elizabeth Alexander, Kwame Anthony Appiah, Larry and Adele Bacow, Bev Beatty, Patti

Bellinger, David Bindman, Juliet Blake, David Blight, Phoebe Braithwaite, Leslie Brown, Olivia Carpenter, Glenda Carpio, Panashe Chigumadzi, Richard Cohen, Andrew Curran, Persis Drell, Geralyn Dreyfous, Driss Elghannaz, Cynthia Erivo, Ellen Essenfeld, Drew Faust, Henry Finder, Laura Fisher, Eric Foner, Alan Garber, Claudine Gay, Adam Gopnik, Stephen Greenblatt, Emily Greenhouse, Kevin Guiney, Catherine Hall, Sophie Hanson, Patricia Harrison, Bernard Hicks, Lauren Hom, Glenn and Debbie Hutchins, Lucy Jakub, Barbara Johnson, Robin Kelsey, Paula Kerger, Jamaica Kincaid, Jeff Matrician, Dyllan McGee, Giovanna Micconi, W. J. T. Mitchell, Marcyliena Morgan, Dr. Thomas Nash, Terri Oliver, Dawna Phaneuf, David Remnick, Dr. Daniel Richman, Hollis Robbins, Sharon Rockefeller, Jose Sanabria, Sharmila Sen, Sara Serlen, Tommie Shelby, Ruth Simmons, Michael D. Smith, Robert F. Smith, Georgia Soares, John Stauffer, Claude Steele, Sabin Streeter, Jim and Susan Swartz, Maria Tatar, Helen Vendler, Darren Walker, Natalia Warchol, and Mark Weigel.

Finally, I am grateful for the gift of my family: my stepdaughter, Cristina Suarez, and her husband, Reinier Bao; my stepson Jose Suarez and his fiancée, Jessica Cruz; my stepson Jesus Suarez and his fiancée, Rocio Rives; my daughter Liza Gates; my daughter Maggie Gates and her husband, my son-in-law, Aaron Hatley, and their beautiful daughter, my granddaughter, Eleanor Margaret Gates-Hatley; and of course my brilliant wife, Dr. Marial Iglesias Utset, my most searching critic and my staunchest supporter.

Notes

Preface: The Black Box

1. Martin Robison Delany, *The Condition, Elevation, Emigration, and Destiny of the Colored People of the United States* (Philadelphia: published by the author, 1852), 9, 221; Du Bois quoted in David Levering Lewis and Deborah Willis, *A Small Nation of People: W. E. B. Du Bois and African American Portraits of Progress* (Washington, DC: Library of Congress, 2003), 18.

2. Stephen L. Carter, *Reflections of an Affirmative Action Baby* (New York: Basic Books, 1991), 1.

3. Barbara Johnson, "The Critical Difference," *Diacritics* 8, no. 2 (Summer 1978): 2; Barbara Johnson, *A World of Difference* (Baltimore: The Johns Hopkins University Press, 1987).

4. Henry Box Brown, *Narrative of the Life of Henry Box Brown, Written by Himself* (Manchester, England: Printed by Lee and Glynn, 1851), 53, Documenting the American South, docsouth.unc.edu/neh/brownbox/brownbox.html.

5. Frederick Douglass, *Narrative of the Life of Frederick Douglass, an American Slave. Written by Himself* (Boston: Published at the Anti-Slavery Office, 1845), 13, Documenting the American South, docsouth.unc.edu/neh/douglass/douglass.html.

6. Douglass, *Narrative*, 13.

7. Thomas Wentworth Higginson, "Negro Spirituals," *Atlantic Monthly* 19, no. 116 (June 1867): 685.

8. Douglass, *Narrative*, 14.

9. Bill Egan, "Europe, James Reese," *Oxford African American Studies Center*, doi.org/10.1093/acref/9780195301731.013.45530.

10. Marcus Garvey, "The Negro's Greatest Enemy," *Current History*, Sept. 1923, in *Selected Writings and Speeches of Marcus Garvey*, ed. Bob Blaisdell (Mineola, NY: Dover Publications, 2004), 9. One example of Washington using the crab metaphor was relayed by the *Commercial Advertiser* (Hawaiian Territories) newspaper on May 30, 1904. Here Washington told a fable about an "old colored man" who was unconcerned about his crabs escaping from their box: "I'se a crabologist, I is, and I knows all 'bout de crab nature. I don't need to watch 'em a'tall. When de big crab fights up to de top an' when he is gittin' out, de little crab catches him by de laig and pulls him back. He can't get out nohow." Washington then delivered the ironic punch line: "My friends, I have been informed that there is something of the crab nature in human nature, but it must be altogether among the white folks and not in our race." Black writers continued to use the crab barrel metaphor after Washington. For example, Hubert Harrison relayed the "just-so story" of the crab barrel to criticize Black socialists in Harlem of mounting a "Pull It Down" program. See Hubert Harrison, "Just Crabs," *Negro World*, Mar. 27, 1920, reprinted in *When Africa Awakes* (New York: Porro Press, 1920), 73–75. See also Jeffrey B. Perry, ed., *A Hubert Harrison Reader* (Middletown, CT: Wesleyan University Press, 2021), 109–11.

11. W. E. B. Du Bois, *The Souls of Black Folk* (Chicago: A. C. McClurg & Co., 1903), 1.

12. Du Bois, *The Souls of Black Folk*, 3.

13. See W. E. B. Du Bois, "A Negro Nation Within a Nation," June 26, 1934, blackpast.org/african-american-history/speeches-african-american -history/1934-w-e-b-du-bois-negro-nation-within-nation; W. E. B. Du Bois, "Segregation," *The Crisis* (May 1934): 147; Michael Beschloss, "How an Experiment with Dolls Helped Lead to School Integration," *The New York Times*, May 6, 2014.

14. Alain Locke, "Enter the New Negro," *Survey Graphic*, Mar. 1925; and Alain Locke, ed., *The New Negro: Voices of the Harlem Renaissance* (1925; repr., New York: Touchstone, 1997), 3.

15. W. E. B. Du Bois, *Black Folk Then and Now: An Essay on the History and Sociology of the Negro Race* (1939; repr., New York: Oxford University Press, 2007), xxxii.

16. Terrance Hayes, "The Blue Seuss," in *Wind in a Box* (New York: Penguin, 2006), 43–44.

17. Stephen Menn and Justin E. H. Smith, eds. and trans., *Anton Wilhelm Amo's Philosophical Dissertations of Mind and Body* (New York: Oxford University Press, 2020), 21–22.

18. Susan J. Hubert, "Capitein, Jacobus," Oxford African American Studies Center, doi.org.ezp-prod1.hul.harvard.edu/10.1093/acref/978019530173 1.013.44610.

19. Jos Damen, "Dutch Letters from Ghana," *History Today* 62, no. 8 (Aug. 2012): 47–52.

20. Iris Wigger and Spencer Hadley, "Angelo Soliman: Desecrated Bodies and the Spectre of Enlightenment Racism," *Race and Class* 62, no. 2 (Aug. 3, 2020): 83, doi.org/10.1177/0306396820942470.

21. Wigger and Hadley, "Angelo Soliman," 83.

22. Wigger and Hadley, "Angelo Soliman," 81–82.

Chapter One: Race, Reason, and Writing

1. Statistics from "Trans-Atlantic Slave Trade—Estimates," SlaveVoyages, slavevoyages.org/assessment/estimates.

2. Vincent Carretta, *Phillis Wheatley: Biography of a Genius in Bondage* (Athens: University of Georgia Press, 2011), 1.

3. Carretta, *Phillis Wheatley*, 37, 46, 65–66, 79–81.

4. Carretta, *Phillis Wheatley*, 80–84.

5. Joanna Brooks, "Our Phillis, Ourselves," *American Literature* 82, no. 1 (2010): 1–28; Hollis Robbins, "Examining Phillis Wheatley," *Los Angeles Review of Books*, Dec. 19, 2022.

6. Carretta, *Phillis Wheatley*, 85, 91–100.

7. Lurana Donnels O'Malley, "'Why I Wrote the Phyllis Wheatley Pageant-Play': Mary Church Terrell's Bicentennial Activism," *Theatre History Studies* 37 (2018): 225–55.

8. David Waldstreicher, "The Wheatleyan Moment," *Early American Studies: An Interdisciplinary Journal* 9, no. 3 (Fall 2011): 522–51.

9. Vincent Carretta, *Phillis Wheatley Peters: Biography of a Genius in Bondage* (Athens: University of Georgia Press, 2023), 86.

10. Carretta, *Phillis Wheatley Peters: Biography of a Genius in Bondage*, 226, n49.

11. Vincent Carretta, *The Writings of Phillis Wheatley* (Oxford: Oxford University Press, 2019), 161; James Albert Ukawsaw Gronniosaw, *A Narrative of the Most Remarkable Particulars in the Life of James Albert Ukawsaw Gronniosaw, an African Prince, as Related by Himself* (Bath, England: W. GYE, 1772), Documenting the American South, docsouth.unc.edu/neh /gronniosaw/gronnios.html.

12. Robbins, "Examining Phillis Wheatley."

13. In M. Fontenelle, *Conversations with a Lady on the Plurality of Worlds, to Which Is Also Added a Discourse Concerning the Antients and Moderns*

(London: J. Darby, 1719), 94, 183–84. Translated from the French by Andrew S. Curran.

14. On the Bordeaux essays, see Henry Louis Gates, Jr., and Andrew S. Curran, eds., *Who's Black and Why?: A Hidden Chapter from the Eighteenth-Century Invention of Race* (Cambridge, MA: Harvard University Press, 2022).

15. Footnote quoted in Emmanuel C. Eze, "Hume, Race, and Nature," *Journal of the History of Ideas* 61, no. 4 (Oct. 2000): 691–98.

16. Immanuel Kant, *Observations on the Feeling of the Beautiful and Sublime*, trans. John T. Goldthwait (Berkeley: University of California Press, 1960), 110–11.

17. Montesquieu, *De l'esprit des lois* (Paris: Garnier frères, 1973), 1:248; Montesquieu, *Pensées et fragments inédits de Montesquieu* (Bordeaux, France: G. Gounouilhou, 1889), 167. Both sources translated from the French by Andrew S. Curran.

18. Quoted in Andrew S. Curran, *The Anatomy of Blackness: Science and Slavery in an Age of Enlightenment* (Baltimore: Johns Hopkins University Press, 2011), 14.

19. Edward D. Seeber, "Phillis Wheatley," *The Journal of Negro History*, vol. 24, no. 3 (Jul. 1939): 260.

20. All Jefferson quotations from Excerpt of Thomas Jefferson, *Notes on the State of Virginia*, Africans in America, pbs.org/wgbh/aia/part3/3h490t .html.

21. Henry Louis Gates, Jr., and Andrew S. Curran, "We Need a New Language for Talking About Race," *The New York Times*, Mar. 3, 2022, nytimes.com/2022/03/03/opinion/sunday/talking-about-race.html.

22. Nina Jablonski, "What Is It About Skin Color?," *The Root*, Feb. 16, 2013, theroot.com/what-is-it-about-skin-color-1790895168.

23. See my response to Sean Wilentz's "Who Lincoln Was" in *The New Republic*, July 25, 2009, newrepublic.com/article/63777/disputations-the -lost-lincoln-0.

24. Georg Wilhelm Friedrich Hegel, *The Philosophy of History*, rev. ed., trans. John Sibree (New York: Wiley Book Co., 1900), 99.

25. Morgan Godwyn, *The Negro's and Indians Advocate, Suing for Their Admission into the Church* (London, 1680), 13.

26. Stephen Menn and Justin E. H. Smith explain that there is significant evidence suggesting that Amo was not enslaved. They write, "As scholars have generally agreed since the work of Norbert Lochner in the 1950s, if Amo had not been transported to Europe with the agreement of his parents, it is unlikely that his family name would have been known upon

arrival ('Amo' and its variants are common in the Akan-speaking world), and just as unlikely that he would have known where to return to, as he eventually does late in life after a long career in Germany. . . . Beyond the reasonable presumption that Amo spent his years in Germany with knowledge of his family origins, there is significant uncertainty about the circumstances of Amo's arrival in Europe." See the introduction to Menn and Smith, *Anton Wilhelm Amo's Philosophical Dissertations on Mind and Body*, 4.

27. Grant Parker, "Capitein, Jacobus Elisa Johannes," Oxford African American Studies Center, doi.org.ezp-prod1.hul.harvard.edu/10.1093/acref /9780195301731.013.48495; Susan J. Hubert, "Capitein, Jacobus," Oxford African American Studies Center, doi.org.ezp-prod1.hul.harvard .edu/10.1093/acref/9780195301731.013.44610.

28. Alexander Crummell, "The Attitude of the American Mind Toward the Negro Intellect," blackpast.org/african-american-history/1898-alexander -crummell-attitude-american-mind-toward-negro-intellect.

29. David W. Blight, *Frederick Douglass: Prophet of Freedom* (New York: Simon and Schuster, 2018), 487.

30. Henry Louis Gates, Jr., and William L. Andrews, *Pioneers of the Black Atlantic: Five Slave Narratives from the Enlightenment, 1772–1815* (Washington, DC: Civitas, 1998), 10–11.

31. Gronniosaw, *A Narrative of the Most Remarkable Particulars in the Life of James Albert Ukawsaw Gronniosaw, an African Prince, as Related by Himself.*

32. See Henry Louis Gates, Jr., *100 Amazing Facts About the Negro* (New York: Pantheon, 2017), chapter 64.

33. "Banneker's Letter to Jefferson," Africans in America, PBS, pbs.org/wgbh /aia/part2/2h71t.html.

34. "Agriculture and Slavery in the South," in *Major Problems in American History*, vol. 1, eds. Elizabeth Cobbs and Edward J. Blum (Boston: Cengage, 2017), 335; Sven Beckert, *Empire of Cotton: A Global History* (New York: Vintage Books, 2014), 243.

35. David Walker, *Walker's Appeal, in Four Articles; Together with a Preamble, to the Coloured Citizens of the World, but in Particular, and Very Expressly, to Those of the United States of America, Written in Boston, State of Massachusetts, September 28, 1829*, 3rd ed. (Boston: David Walker, 1839), 17–18, Documenting the American South, docsouth.unc.edu/nc/walker/walker .html.

36. *New York Tribune*, "Frederick Douglass Dead," Feb. 21, 1895, 1, as quoted in Blight, *Frederick Douglass: Prophet of Freedom*, 756.

37. Frederick Douglass, "The Claims of the Negro, Ethnologically Considered," in *The Portable Frederick Douglass*, eds. John Stauffer and Henry Louis Gates, Jr. (New York: Penguin, 2016), 223–47. Also in Philip S. Foner and Yuval Taylor, eds., *Frederick Douglass: Selected Speeches and Writings* (Chicago: Lawrence Hill Books, 1999), 283–88.

Chapter Two: What's in a Name?

1. Ben L. Martin, "From Negro to Black to African American: The Power of Names and Naming," *Political Science Quarterly* 106, no. 1 (Spring 1991): 83.

2. James McCune Smith, "On the Fourteenth Query of Thomas Jefferson's *Notes on Virginia*," *Anglo-African Magazine* (Aug. 1859), in *The Voice of Black America: Major Speeches by Blacks in the United States 1797–1973*, vol. 1, ed. Philip S. Foner (New York: Capricorn Books, 1975), 237–48.

3. McCune Smith, "On the Fourteenth Query of Thomas Jefferson's *Notes on Virginia*," 247.

4. *Freedom's Journal*, Apr. 4, 1828.

5. Dorothy Sterling, *Speak Out in Thunder Tones: Letters and Other Writings by Black Northerners, 1787–1865* (New York: Doubleday, 1973), 58.

6. Chernoh M. Sesay, "Hall, Prince," Oxford African American Studies Center, doi.org/10.1093/acref/9780195301731.013.34429; Danielle Allen, "A Forgotten Black Founding Father: Why I've Made It My Mission to Teach Others About Prince Hall," *The Atlantic*, Mar. 2021, theatlantic .com/magazine/archive/2021/03/prince-hall-forgotten-founder/617791; Chernoh M. Sesay, Jr., "The Dialectic of Representation: Black Freemasonry, the Black Public, and Black Historiography," *Journal of African American Studies* 17 (Sept. 2013): 380–98.

7. Sesay, "Hall, Prince"; "Emigration and Colonization: The Debate Among African Americans, 1780s–1860s," National Humanities Center Resource Toolbox, *The Making of African Identity*, vol. 1, 1500–1865, na tionalhumanitiescenter.org/pds/maai/identity/text10/emigrationcoloni zation.pdf; "Prince Hall Freemasonry: A Resource Guide," Library of Congress Research Guides, guides.loc.gov/prince-hall-freemasonry.

8. Donald R. Wright, "Cuffe, Paul," *African American National Biography*, Oxford African American Studies Center, doi.org.ezp-prod1.hul.har vard.edu/10.1093/acref/9780195301731.013.34327; Lamont D. Thomas, "Cuffe, Paul," *American National Biography Online*, anb.org/view/10.1093 /anb/9780198606697.001.0001/anb-9780198606697-e-1500980.

9. Wright, "Cuffe, Paul"; Thomas, "Cuffe, Paul."

10. "Blacks Petition Against Taxation Without Representation, March 14, 1780," sageamericanhistory.net/federalperiod/docs/BlacksPet.htm.

11. Wright, "Cuffe, Paul"; Thomas, "Cuffe, Paul."

12. Wright, "Cuffe, Paul"; Thomas, "Cuffe, Paul."

13. James T. Campbell, *Middle Passages: African American Journeys to Africa, 1775–2005* (New York: Penguin Books, 2007).

14. James Forten, "Letter to Paul Cuffee [1817]," in *Call and Response: Key Debates in African American Studies*, eds. Henry Louis Gates, Jr., and Jennifer Burton (New York: W. W. Norton and Company, 2011), 53.

15. James Forten and Russell Parrott, "Address to the Humane and Benevolent Inhabitants of the City and County of Philadelphia [1818]," in Gates and Burton, *Call and Response*, 54–56.

16. *The Liberator*, Mar. 12, 1831, quoted in William Lloyd Garrison, *Thoughts on African Colonization*, part II (Boston: Garrison and Knapp, 1832), 69.

17. Eddie S. Glaude, Jr., *Exodus!: Religion, Race, and Nation in Early Nineteenth-Century Black America* (Chicago: University of Chicago Press, 2000), 112.

18. Howard Holman Bell, *A Survey of the Negro Convention Movement, 1830–1861* (New York: Arno Press, 1969). The Arno Press edition is a reprint of Bell's 1953 PhD dissertation at Northwestern.

19. Glaude, *Exodus!*, 113; Bell, *A Survey of the Negro Convention Movement, 1830–1861*, 12–13; P. Gabrielle Foreman, "Black Organizing, Print Advocacy, and Collective Authorship: The Long History of the Colored Conventions Movement," in *The Colored Conventions Movement: Black Organizing in the Nineteenth Century*, eds. P. Gabrielle Foreman, Jim Casey, and Sarah Lynn Patterson (Chapel Hill: University of North Carolina Press, 2021), 21, 26; Woodson quote from "Emergency in Cincinnati: The Origins of the 1830 Convention: The Meeting That Launched a Movement: The First National Convention," Colored Conventions Project, coloredconventions.org/first-convention/origins-1830-convention /emergency-in-cincinnati.

20. "Other Precursors to the Convention Movement," Colored Conventions Project, coloredconventions.org/first-convention/origins-1830-convention /other-precursors.

21. Glaude, *Exodus!*, 113.

22. Jim Casey, "Social Networks of the Colored Conventions, 1830–1864," in Foreman, Casey, and Patterson, *The Colored Conventions Movement*, 268–77; Jeffrey A. Mullins, "National Conventions of Colored Men," *Encyclopedia of African American History*, doi.org/10.1093/acref/9780195 301731.013.44911.

23. "Traditional Elements: The Conventions of Conventions: Political Rituals and Traditions," Colored Conventions Project, coloredconventions .org/Black-political-practices/rituals-and-routines/traditional-elements.

24. Foreman, "Black Organizing, Print Advocacy, and Collective Authorship," 29.

25. "Letter V by Long Island Scribe," *The Colored American*, Colored Conventions Project, omeka.coloredconventions.org/items/show/750.

26. Casey, "Social Networks of the Colored Conventions, 1830–1864," 263–65; Bell, *A Survey of the Negro Convention Movement, 1830–1861*, 27.

27. Glaude, *Exodus!*, 113.

28. Martha S. Jones, *Birthright Citizens: A History of Race and Rights in Antebellum America* (New York: Cambridge University Press, 2018), 37–40; "Traditional Origin Story: The Meeting That Launched a Movement: The First National Convention," Colored Conventions Project, colored conventions.org/first-convention/origins-1830-convention/traditional-origin-story; Bell, *A Survey of the Negro Convention Movement, 1830–1861*, 13–16; Richard S. Newman, *Freedom's Prophet: Bishop Richard Allen, the AME Church, and the Black Founding Fathers* (New York: New York University Press, 2008), 6, 21.

29. "The Convention Event," Colored Conventions Project, coloredconventions.org/first-convention/the-convention-event.

30. Bell, *A Survey of the Negro Convention Movement, 1830–1861*, 16; Foreman, "Black Organizing, Print Advocacy, and Collective Authorship," 26.

31. "Constitution of the American Society of Free Persons of Colour, for Improving Their Condition in the United States; for Purchasing Lands; and for the Establishment of a Settlement in Upper Canada, Also, the Proceedings of the Convention with Their Address to Free Persons of Colour in the United States," Colored Conventions Project, omeka.col oredconventions.org/items/show/70.

32. "Freedom's Journal," PBS, pbs.org/Blackpress/news_bios/newbios/nwsppr /freedom/freedom.html.

33. All quotations from the 1831 convention are from "Minutes and Proceedings of the First Annual Convention of the People of Colour, Held by Adjournments in the City of Philadelphia, from the Sixth to the Eleventh of June, Inclusive, 1831," Colored Conventions Project, https:// omeka.coloredconventions.org/items/show/72.

34. Glaude, *Exodus!*, 190, n27.

35. Sterling, *Speak Out in Thunder Tones*, 61.

36. Walker, *Walker's Appeal*, 61, quoted in Sterling, *Speak Out in Thunder Tones*, 61.

37. *The Liberator*, June 4, 1831, quoted in Sterling, *Speak Out in Thunder Tones*, 61.

38. *The Liberator*, Sept. 24, 1831, quoted in Sterling, *Speak Out in Thunder Tones*, 61–62.

39. *The Liberator*, Sept. 24, 1831, quoted in Sterling, *Speak Out in Thunder Tones*, 62.

40. *The Colored American*, Mar. 4, 1837, quoted in Sterling, *Speak Out in Thunder Tones*, 62–63.

41. Glaude, *Exodus!*, 127.

42. Joan L. Bryant, "Colored Conventions, Moral Reform, and the American Race Problem," in Foreman, Casey, and Patterson, *The Colored Conventions Movement*, 169.

43. Glaude, *Exodus!*, 132–33.

44. Glaude, *Exodus!*, 135–36.

45. Bryant, "Colored Conventions, Moral Reform, and the American Race Problem," 171.

46. Glaude, *Exodus!*, 139.

47. Sidney, "Letter to the Editor [1841]," in Gates and Burton, *Call and Response*, 93–95; "The Colored American," Mar. 6, 13, 1841, *The Liberator*, quoted in Sterling, *Speak Out in Thunder Tones*, 61; Glaude, *Exodus!*, 140–42.

48. "The Colored American," Mar. 6, 13, 1841, *The Liberator*, quoted in Sterling, *Speak Out in Thunder Tones*, 61.

49. Milton C. Sernett, "Garnet, Henry Highland," *American National Biography Online*, doi.org/10.1093/anb/9780198606697.article.1500253.

50. Garnet quotations from "Garnet's 'Call to Rebellion,'" PBS, pbs.org/wgbh/aia/part4/4h2937t.html; David W. Blight, *Frederick Douglass: Prophet of Freedom* (New York: Simon and Schuster, 2018), 133.

51. Sernett, "Garnet, Henry Highland"; Frances Smith Foster, "Garnet, Henry Highland," *African American National Biography*, Oxford African American Studies Center, doi.org.ezp-prod1.hul.harvard.edu/10.1093/acref/9780195301731.013.34403.

52. Quoted in Cheryl Janifer LaRoche, *Free Black Communities and the Underground Railroad: The Geography of Resistance* (Urbana: University of Illinois Press, 2014), xiii.

Chapter Three: Who's Your Daddy?: Frederick Douglass and the Politics of Self-Representation

1. David W. Blight, *Frederick Douglass: Prophet of Freedom* (New York: Simon and Schuster, 2018), 87.

2. Frederick Douglass, *Narrative of the Life of Frederick Douglass, an American Slave. Written by Himself* (Boston: Published at the Anti-Slavery Of-

fice, 1845), 112, Documenting the American South, docsouth.unc.edu /neh/douglass/douglass.html.

3. Booker T. Washington, *Up from Slavery: An Autobiography* (Garden City, NY: Doubleday, 1901), 23–24, Documenting the American South, doc south.unc.edu/fpn/washington/washing.html.

4. John Jea, *The Life, History, and Unparalleled Sufferings of John Jea, the African Preacher. Compiled and Written by Himself* (Portsea, England: 1811), 34–36, Documenting the American South, docsouth.unc.edu/neh/jeajohn /jeajohn.html.

5. Douglass, *Narrative*, 33.

6. Ishmael Reed, *Flight to Canada* (New York: Random House, 1976), 14.

7. Amanda B. Page, Summary, *Narrative of James Williams*, Documenting the American South, docsouth.unc.edu/fpn/williams/summary.html; Carrie Spell, *Encyclopedia of Alabama*.

8. Hank Trent, ed., *Narrative of James Williams, An American Slave, Annotated Edition* (Baton Rouge: Louisiana State University Press, 2013), xv–xviii.

9. Trent, *Narrative of James Williams, An American Slave, Annotated Edition*, ix–xxix.

10. Portions of the Douglass material in this chapter have appeared before in my essays "Binary Oppositions in Chapter One of *Narrative of the Life of Frederick Douglass*," in *Afro-American Literature: The Reconstruction of Instruction*, eds. Dexter Fisher and Robert B. Stepto (New York: Modern Language Association of America, 1978), 212–32; and "Frederick Douglass's Camera Obscura: Representing the Antislave 'Clothed and in Their Own Form,'" *Critical Inquiry* 42, no. 1 (Autumn 2015): 31–60.

11. James McCune Smith, "Introduction," in Frederick Douglass, *My Bondage and My Freedom* (New York: Miller, Orton & Mulligan, 1855), 25, Documenting the American South, docsouth.unc.edu/neh/douglass55/doug lass55.html.

12. John Stauffer, Zoe Trodd, and Celeste-Marie Bernier, *Picturing Frederick Douglass: An Illustrated Biography of the Nineteenth Century's Most Photographed American* (New York: Liveright, 2015).

13. Peter F. Walker, *Moral Choices: Memory, Desire, and Imagination in Nineteenth-Century American Abolition* (Baton Rouge: Louisiana State University Press, 1978), 209–11, 229–36.

14. Walker, *Moral Choices*, 209–11, 229–36.

15. *New York Times*, Feb. 21, 1895.

16. Douglass, *Narrative*, 1–2.

17. Douglass, *Narrative*, 65–66.

18. Douglass, *Narrative*, 1–5.

19. Douglass, *My Bondage and My Freedom*, 52.

20. Frederick Douglass, *Life and Times of Frederick Douglass* (Hartford, CT: Park Publishing Co., 1881), 15, Documenting the American South, doc south.unc.edu/neh/douglasslife/douglass.html.

21. Douglass, *My Bondage and My Freedom*, 55–56.

22. Douglass, *My Bondage and My Freedom*, 57–58.

23. Walker, *Moral Choices*, 252.

24. Frederick Douglass, "The Claims of the Negro, Ethnologically Considered," in *The Portable Frederick Douglass*, eds. John Stauffer and Henry Louis Gates, Jr. (New York: Penguin, 2016), 235.

25. From DNA research, we know today that 35 percent of all African American males today can trace their y-DNA, their male ancestry, back to a white man, and the average African American, male or female, can trace 24 percent or so of their DNA to European ancestry.

Chapter Four: Who's Your Mama?: The Politics of Disrespectability

1. Evelyn Brooks Higginbotham, *Righteous Discontent: The Women's Movement in the Black Baptist Church, 1880–1920* (Cambridge, MA: Harvard University Press, 1994); see also Rayford W. Logan, *The Betrayal of the Negro, from Rutherford B. Hayes to Woodrow Wilson* (New York: Collier Books, 1954; 1965), 52.

2. Walter F. Willcox, "The Negro Population," in Walter F. Willcox and W. E. B. Du Bois, *Negroes in the United States* (Washington, DC: Bureau of the Census, 1904), 11–13, www2.census.gov/prod2/decennial/docu ments/03322287no8ch1.pdf.

3. "Segregation and Disfranchisement," Digital History (University of Houston), digitalhistory.uh.edu/disp_textbook.cfm?smtid=2&psid=3182; "Whites Only: Jim Crow in America," Separate Is Not Equal: Brown v. Board of Education, Smithsonian National Museum of American History, americanhistory.si.edu/brown/history/1-segregated/white-only-1 .html; Sylviane A. Diouf, *Dreams of Africa in Alabama: The Slave Ship Clotilda and the Story of the Last Africans Brought to America* (New York: Oxford University Press, 2007), 209.

4. "Booker T. Washington Delivers the 1895 Atlanta Compromise Speech," History Matters, historymatters.gmu.edu/d/39.

5. "Booker T. Washington Delivers the 1895 Atlanta Compromise Speech," History Matters.

6. Booker T. Washington, *Up from Slavery: An Autobiography* (Garden City, NY: Doubleday, 1901), 81, Documenting the American South, docsouth .unc.edu/fpn/washington/washing.html.

7. David Levering Lewis, *W. E. B. Du Bois: Biography of a Race, 1868–1919* (New York: Owl Books, 1993), 175.

8. Higginbotham, *Righteous Discontent*, 145, 269, n71.

9. *Hartford Daily Courant*, Jan. 8, 1887; *Washington Bee*, Feb. 19, 1887.

10. *Chicago Inter-Ocean*, Oct. 2, 1895.

11. *Cleveland Gazette*, June 28, 1895.

12. David Levering Lewis, "A Small Nation of People: W. E. B. Du Bois and Black Americans at the Turn of the Twentieth Century," in Library of Congress, *A Small Nation of People: W. E. B. Du Bois and African American Portraits of Progress* (New York: Amistad, 2003), location 192–202 of 1298, Kindle.

13. Lewis, "A Small Nation of People," location 113 of 1289, Kindle.

14. W. E. B. Du Bois, "The American Negro at Paris," *American Monthly Review of Reviews* 22, no. 5 (Nov. 1900): 575–77, webdubois.org/dbANParis.html.

15. Lewis, "A Small Nation of People," locations 126, 236 of 1289, Kindle.

16. Deborah Willis, "The Sociologist's Eye: W. E. B. Du Bois and the Paris Exposition," in Library of Congress, *A Small Nation of People: W. E. B. Du Bois and African American Portraits of Progress* (New York: Amistad, 2003), location 710 of 1289, Kindle.

17. "Advertisements for Madam C. J. Walker's Products," National Museum of African American History and Culture, Smithsonian Institution, nmaahc.si.edu/object/nmaahc_2013.153.11.1.

18. "Signifying Monkey," in Bruce Jackson, *Get Your Ass in the Water and Swim Like Me: African American Narrative Poetry from Oral Tradition* (1974; repr., London: Routledge, 2017), 169.

19. "Titanic," in Jackson, *Get Your Ass in the Water and Swim Like Me*, 190.

20. Jackson, preface to *Get Your Ass in the Water and Swim Like Me*, viii.

21. See Claudia Mitchell-Kernan, *Language Behavior in a Black Urban Community* (Berkeley: University of California Press, 1971); and "Signifying, Loud-Talking and Marking (1972)," in *Signifyin(g), Sanctifyin', and Slam Dunking: A Reader in African American Expressive Culture*, ed. Gena Dagel Caponi (Amherst: University of Massachusetts Press, 1999).

22. Zora Neale Hurston, *Their Eyes Were Watching God* (1937; repr., New York: Harper & Row, 1990), 75.

23. Jean Toomer, "The *Cane* Years," in *The Wayward and the Seeking: A Collection of Writings by Jean Toomer*, ed. Darwin T. Turner (Washington, DC: Howard University Press, 1980), 123.

24. Daniel Alexander Payne, *Recollections of Seventy Years* (New York: Arno Press and The New York Times, 1969), 253–54.

25. Portions of my discussions of Black folklore have appeared in my essay "The Politics of 'Negro Folklore,'" which was published as the foreword to *The Annotated African American Folktales*, eds. Henry Louis Gates, Jr., and Maria Tatar (New York: Liveright, 2017), xxiii–lii.

26. Charles W. Chesnutt, "The Goophered Grapevine," *Atlantic Monthly* 60 (Aug. 1887): 259–60.

27. Charles W. Chesnutt, *The Conjure Woman* (Durham, NC: Duke University Press, 1993).

28. Charles W. Chesnutt, "Superstitions and Folk-lore of the South," *Modern Culture* 13 (May 1901): 231.

29. Chesnutt, "Superstitions and Folk-lore of the South," 231.

30. Charles W. Chesnutt, "Post-Bellum Pre Harlem," *Colophon* 2.5 (Feb. 1931).

31. Sterling A. Brown, "Folk Literature," in *A Son's Return* (Boston: Northeastern University Press, 1996), 226.

32. Sterling A. Brown, "Negro Folk Expression," *Phylon* 11.4 (1950): 318.

33. Sterling A. Brown, "Folk Literature," in *Negro Caravan*, eds. Sterling A. Brown, Arthur Paul Davis, and Ulysses Lee (New York: Dryden Press, 1941), 433.

34. Brown, "Negro Folk Expression," 322.

35. Brown, "Folk Literature," 433.

36. Brown, "Folk Literature," 431.

37. Charles W. Chesnutt, *The Marrow of Tradition* (Boston: Houghton Mifflin, 1901), 60–61, Documenting the American South, docsouth.unc.edu/southlit/chesnuttmarrow/chesmarrow.html.

38. W. E. B. Du Bois, "The Talented Tenth," in *The Negro Problem: A Series of Articles by Representative American Negroes of To-day* (New York: James Pott & Co., 1903), 45.

39. W. E. B. Du Bois, *The Souls of Black Folk* (Chicago: A. C. McClurg & Co., 1903), 38.

40. W. E. B. Du Bois, *The Philadelphia Negro: A Social Study* (1899; repr., New York: Oxford University Press, 2007), 225.

41. Lewis, "A Small Nation of People," location 168–78 of 1289, Kindle.

42. Du Bois, *The Philadephia Negro*, 225.

Chapter Five: The "True Art of a Race's Past": Art, Propaganda, and the New Negro

1. David Levering Lewis, "Dr. Johnson's Friends: Civil Rights by Copyright During Harlem's Mid-Twenties," *Massachusetts Review* 20, no. 3 (Autumn 1979): 501–19.

2. Steve Kramer, "Matthews, Victoria Earle," *American National Biography Online*, doi.org/10.1093/anb/9780198606697.article.1501315; Floris Barnett Cash, "Matthews, Victoria Earle," *African American National Biography*, Oxford African American Studies Center, doi.org.ezp-prod1.hul .harvard.edu/10.1093/acref/9780195301731.013.34570.

3. Kramer, "Matthews, Victoria Earle"; Cash, "Matthews, Victoria Earle."

4. Val Marie Johnson, "'The Half Has Never Been Told': Maritcha Lyons' Community, Black Women Educators, the Woman's Loyal Union, and 'the Color Line' in Progressive Era Brooklyn and New York," *Journal of Urban History* 44, no. 5 (2018): 835, 838; Kramer, "Matthews, Victoria Earle."

5. Victoria Earle Matthews, "The Value of Race Literature: An Address Delivered at the First Congress of Colored Women of the United States," in *The Portable Nineteenth-Century African American Women Writers*, eds. Hollis Robbins and Henry Louis Gates, Jr. (New York: Penguin Books, 2017), 505.

6. Matthews, "The Value of Race Literature," 507.

7. Matthews, "The Value of Race Literature," 507–8.

8. Matthews, "The Value of Race Literature," 507.

9. Matthews, "The Value of Race Literature," 510.

10. John Y. Cole, "Daniel Murray: A Collector's Legacy," Library of Congress, loc.gov/collections/african-american-perspectives-rare-books/articles -and-essays/daniel-murray-a-collectors-legacy.

11. Quoted in Henry Louis Gates, Jr., and Gene Andrew Jarrett, "Introduction," in *The New Negro: Readings on Race, Representation, and African American Culture, 1892–1938*, eds. Henry Louis Gates, Jr., and Gene Andrew Jarrett (Princeton, NJ: Princeton University Press, 2007), 1.

12. US Census, "Historical Statistics of the United States, 1789–1945," "Population—Race by Regions: 1790 to 1940," Series B, 48–71, "Population Characteristics and Migration," www2.census.gov/library/publications /1949/compendia/hist_stats_1789-1945/hist_stats_1789-1945-chB.pdf.

13. Andrew A. Beveridge, David Halle, Edward Telles, and Beth Leavenworth DuFault, "Residential Diversity and Division: Separation and Segregation Among Whites, Blacks, Hispanics, Asians, Affluent, and Poor," in *New York and Los Angeles: The Uncertain Future*, eds. David Halle and Andrew A. Beveridge (New York: Oxford University Press, 2013), 320.

14. Charles S. Johnson, "The New Frontage on American Life," in *The New Negro*, ed. Alain Locke (1925; repr., New York: Touchstone, 1997), 291.

15. A. Philip Randolph and Chandler Owen, "The New Negro—What Is

He?," *Messenger*, Aug. 1920, in *The Harlem Renaissance: A Brief History with Documents*, ed. Jeffrey B. Ferguson (Boston: Bedford/St. Martin's, 2008), 39–42.

16. Marcus Garvey, "The New Negro and the U.N.I.A. (1919)," in Gates and Jarrett, *The New Negro*, 94.

17. James Weldon Johnson, preface to *The Book of American Negro Poetry* (1922), in Gates and Jarrett, *The New Negro*, 427.

18. Quoted in Wallace Thurman, "Negro Poets and Their Poetry (1928)," in Gates and Jarrett, *The New Negro*, 420.

19. W. E. B. Du Bois, "Criteria of Negro Art," *The Crisis* 32 (Oct. 1926), webdubois.org/dbCriteriaNArt.html.

20. Du Bois, "Criteria of Negro Art."

21. "The Harlem Renaissance: George Schuyler Argues Against 'Black Art,'" History Matters, historymatters.gmu.edu/d/5129.

22. Langston Hughes, "The Negro Artist and the Racial Mountain," *The Nation*, June 23, 1926, thenation.com/article/archive/negro-artist-and-racial -mountain.

23. Hughes, "The Negro Artist and the Racial Mountain."

24. J. A. Rogers, "Jazz at Home," in Locke, *The New Negro*, 224.

25. See my essay "The Politics of 'Negro Folklore,'" which was published as the foreword to *The Annotated African American Folktales*, eds. Henry Louis Gates, Jr., and Maria Tatar (New York: Liveright, 2017), xxiii–lii.

26. Lee D. Baker, *Anthropology and the Racial Politics of Culture* (Durham, NC: Duke University Press, 2010), 33–34.

27. Baker, *Anthropology and the Racial Politics of Culture*, 50.

28. Thomas W. Talley, *Negro Folk Rhymes (Wise and Otherwise)* (1922; repr., Knoxville: University of Tennessee Press, 1991); Elsie Clews Parsons, *Folk-Lore of the Sea Islands, South Carolina* (Cambridge, MA: American Folk-Lore Society, 1923).

29. Arthur Huff Fauset, "Negro Folk Tales from the South (Alabama, Mississippi, Louisiana)," in Locke, *The New Negro*, 238–44.

30. Arthur Huff Fauset, *Black Gods of the Metropolis* (1931; repr., Philadelphia: University of Pennsylvania Press, 2002).

31. Fauset, "Negro Folk Tales," 238.

32. Tanika JoAnn Beamon, "A History of African American Folklore Scholarship," PhD diss., University of California, Berkeley (2001), 46.

33. Fauset, "Negro Folk Tales," 238–41.

34. Arna Bontemps, "Why I Returned," in *Black Voices: An Anthology of Afro-American Literature*, ed. Abraham Chapman (1968; repr., New York: Signet, 2001), 309–10.

35. Melville J. Herskovits, "The Negro's Americanism," in Locke, *The New Negro*, 353–60.

36. Melville J. Herskovits, "The Negro in the New World: The Statement of a Problem," *American Anthropologist* 32:1 (Jan.–Mar. 1930): 149–50, jstor .org/stable/661054.

37. Melville J. Herskovits, *The Myth of the Negro Past* (1941; repr., Boston: Beacon Press, 1990).

38. E. Franklin Frazier, *The Negro Family in the United States* (Notre Dame, IN: University of Notre Dame Press, 1939).

39. E. Franklin Frazier, "Is the Negro Family a Unique Sociological Unit?," *Opportunity* 5 (June 1927): 166.

40. Baker, *Anthropology and the Racial Politics of Culture*, 13.

41. Ronald Wardhaugh, *An Introduction to Sociolinguistics* (Malden, MA: Blackwell Publishers, 2010), 79.

42. Herbert Aptheker, *American Negro Slave Revolts* (1943; repr., New York: International Publishers, 1978), 64.

43. Robert E. Park, "The Conflict and Fusion of Cultures with Special Reference to the Negro," *Journal of Negro History* 4, no. 2 (Apr. 1919): 117, doi.org/10.2307/2713533.

44. Frazier, *The Negro Family in the United States*, 7–8.

45. Park, "The Conflict and Fusion," 117, quoted in Frazier, *The Negro Family in the United States*, 8.

46. Park, "The Conflict and Fusion," 117, quoted in Frazier, *The Negro Family in the United States*, 8.

47. A. C. Carmichael, *Domestic Manners and Social Condition of the White, Coloured and Negro Population of the West Indies*, vol. I (London: Whittaker and Co., 1834), 251–52.

48. Carmichael, *Domestic Manners and Social Condition of the White, Coloured and Negro Population of the West Indies*, 251–52; Park, "The Conflict and Fusion," 117, quoted in Frazier, *The Negro Family in the United States*, 8.

49. David Eltis, email to author, Aug. 10, 2016.

50. Jean Toomer, "Natalie Mann," in *The Wayward and the Seeking: A Collection of Writings by Jean Toomer*, ed. Darwin T. Turner (Washington, DC: Howard University Press, 1980), 290.

Chapter Six: Modernism and Its Discontents: Zora Neale Hurston and Richard Wright Play the Dozens

1. W. E. B. Du Bois, *The Souls of Black Folk* (Chicago: A. C. McClurg & Co., 1903), viii.

2. Du Bois, *The Souls of Black Folk*, 3.

3. Ralph Waldo Emerson, "The Transcendentalist: A Lecture Read at the Masonic Temple, Boston, January 1842," in *The Prose Works of Ralph Waldo Emerson*, vol. 1, rev. ed. (Boston: Fields, Osgood & Co., 1870), 191.

4. Alfred Binet, *On Double Consciousness: Experimental Psychological Studies* (Chicago: The Open Court Publishing Company, 1890), 77.

5. William James, *The Principles of Psychology*, Volume II (New York: Henry Holt and Company, 1918), 598–602.

6. Du Bois, *The Souls of Black Folk*, 3, 202.

7. Richard Wright, "Between Laughter and Tears," *New Masses*, Oct. 5, 1937, 25.

8. Zora Neale Hurston, Review of *Uncle Tom's Children*, in *Folklore, Memoirs, and Other Writings* (Washington, DC: Library of America, 1995), 912–13.

9. Richard Wright, *Native Son* (London: Victor Gollancz, 1940), 133.

10. Wright, *Native Son*, 265.

11. Ralph Ellison, *Invisible Man* (1952; repr., New York: Vintage Books, 1989), 576–77.

12. "Folk Literature," in *Negro Caravan*, eds. Sterling A. Brown, Arthur Paul Davis, and Ulysses Lee (New York: Dryden Press, 1941), 433.

13. Richard Wright, "Blueprint for Negro Writing," in *African American Literary Theory: A Reader*, ed. Winston Napier (New York: New York University Press, 2000), 47–48.

14. Ralph Ellison, "A Very Stern Discipline," *Harper's* 234 (Mar. 1967): 80.

15. Zora Neale Hurston, "Characteristics of Negro Expression," in Napier, *African American Literary Theory: A Reader*, 36.

16. Toni Morrison, "Rootedness: The Ancestor as Foundation," in *Black Women Writers (1950–1980): A Critical Evaluation*, ed. Mari Evans (New York: Doubleday, 1984), 340–41.

17. Henry James, "The Figure in the Carpet," in *Embarrassments* (New York: Macmillan, 1896).

Chapter Seven: Sellouts vs. Race Men: On the Concept of Passing

1. W. E. B. Du Bois, "*The Drop Sinister*: After the Painting by Harry W. Watrous," *The Crisis* 10, no. 6 (Oct. 1915): 286.

2. James Weldon Johnson, *The Autobiography of an Ex-Colored Man* (Boston: Sherman, French and Company, 1912), 14–17.

3. Johnson, *The Autobiography of an Ex-Colored Man*, 206–7.

NOTES

4. W. E. B. Du Bois, *The Souls of Black Folk* (Chicago: A. C. McClurg & Co., 1903), 4–6.

5. Du Bois, *The Souls of Black Folk*, 202.

6. Paul Lawrence [*sic*] Dunbar, "We Wear the Mask," in *Majors and Minors: Poems* (Toledo, OH: Hadley & Hadley, 1895), 21.

7. Du Bois, *The Souls of Black Folk*, 80.

8. Henry Morehouse, "The Talented Tenth," *The American Missionary* 50, no. 6 (June 1896), gutenberg.org/files/19890/19890-0.txt; Evelyn Brooks Higginbotham, *Righteous Discontent: The Women's Movement in the Black Baptist Church, 1880–1920* (Cambridge, MA: Harvard University Press, 1994). See also Henry Louis Gates, Jr., *100 Amazing Facts About the Negro* (New York: Pantheon, 2017), 54.

9. Robert Kominsky, "We the Americans: Education," United States Bureau of the Census, Sept. 1993, census.gov/prod/cen1990/wepeople/we -11.pdf; Jennifer Cheeseman Day, "88% of Blacks Have a High School Diploma, 26% a Bachelor's Degree," United States Census Bureau, June 10, 2020, census.gov/library/stories/2020/06/Black-high-school-attainment -nearly-on-par-with-national-average.html.

10. W. E. B. Du Bois, "The Talented Tenth," in *The Negro Problem: A Series of Articles by Representative American Negroes of To-day* (New York: James Pott & Co., 1903), 45.

11. Du Bois, "The Talented Tenth," 54.

12. Du Bois, "The Talented Tenth," 75.

13. W. E. B. Du Bois, "The Talented Tenth Memorial Address," in *The Future of the Race*, eds. Henry Louis Gates, Jr., and Cornel West (New York: Vintage Books, 1996), 161–62.

14. Du Bois, "The Talented Tenth Memorial Address," 174.

15. E. Franklin Frazier, *Black Bourgeoisie* (New York: Free Press Paperbacks, 1962), 213.

16. Frazier, *Black Bourgeoisie*, 215–16.

17. Frazier, *Black Bourgeoisie*, 226–27.

18. Frazier, *Black Bourgeoisie*, 230.

19. Frazier, *Black Bourgeoisie*, 227–28.

20. David Levering Lewis, *W. E. B. Du Bois: The Fight for Equality and the American Century, 1919–1963:* (New York: Henry Holt and Company, 2000), 557.

21. Martin Luther King, Jr., "Eulogy for the Young Victims of the 16th Street Baptist Church Bombing," Sept. 18, 1963, mlkscholars.mit.edu /updates/2015/invoking-dr-king.

22. Lewis, *W. E. B. Du Bois: The Fight for Equality and the American Century, 1919–1963*, 334–46, 534.

23. Stuart Hall, "Race, the Floating Signifier: What More Is There to Say About 'Race'?," in *Selected Writings on Race and Difference*, eds. Paul Gilroy and Ruth Wilson Gilmore [1997] (Durham, NC: Duke University Press, 2021), 362.

Conclusion: Policing the Color Line

1. James Baldwin, "Letter from a Region in My Mind," *The New Yorker*, Nov. 9, 1962, newyorker.com/magazine/1962/11/17/letter-from-a-region -in-my-mind.

2. Portions of this conclusion appeared in a guest essay I contributed to *The New York Times* Opinion section in the wake of Florida governor Ron DeSantis's decrying what he called the "agenda" of the College Board's proposed AP African American Studies course. Henry Louis Gates, Jr., "Who's Afraid of Black History?," *The New York Times*, Feb. 17, 2023, nytimes.com/2023/02/17/opinion/desantis-florida-african-american -studies-black-history.html.

3. Danteé Ramos, "DeSantis Says Florida Rejected AP African American Studies Course Because It Includes Study of 'Queer Theory,'" *Yahoo!*, Jan. 24, 2023, yahoo.com/lifestyle/desantis-says-florida-rejected-ap-1830 01870.html.

4. C. Irvine Walker, quoted in Mildred Lewis Rutherford, *A Measuring Rod to Test Text Books, and Reference Books in Schools, Colleges and Libraries*, prepared for the United Confederate Veterans, 1920, 3, online at dlg .galileo.usg.edu/georgiabooks/pdfs/gb5126.pdf.

5. Sarah H. Case, "The Historical Ideology of Mildred Lewis Rutherford: A Confederate Historian's New South Creed," *Journal of Southern History* 68, no. 3 (Aug. 2002): 599–628; Brooks D. Simpson, "Cobb, Howell," *American National Biography Online*, doi.org/10.1093/anb/97801986 06697.article.0300104; Carolyn Terry Bradshaw, "Rutherford, Mildred Lewis," *American National Biography Online*, doi.org/10.1093/anb/9780 198606697.article.0900906; Donald Yacovone, *Teaching White Supremacy: America's Democratic Ordeal and the Forging of Our National Identity* (New York: Pantheon Books, 2022), 346.

6. David W. Blight, *Race and Reunion: The Civil War in American Memory* (Cambridge, MA: The Belknap Press of Harvard University Press, 2002), 279.

7. Yacovone, *Teaching White Supremacy*, 116–17; Mildred Lewis Rutherford, *Mrs. Rutherford's Scrap Book: Valuable Information About the South: The Causes That Led to the War Between the States* (Athens, GA: self-published, 1923), 10.

8. Rutherford, *A Measuring Rod*, 4.

9. Mildred Lewis Rutherford, "The Civilization of the Old South: What Made It: What Destroyed It: What Has Replaced It," in *Miss Rutherford's Scrap Book: Valuable Information About the South: The Assassination of Abraham Lincoln*, vol. 2 (Athens, GA: self-published, 1924), 6.

10. Yacovone, *Teaching White Supremacy*, 269.

11. Mildred Lewis Rutherford, *The South Must Have Her Rightful Place in History* (Athens, GA: self-published, 1923), 18–19.

12. Mildred Lewis Rutherford, *Miss Rutherford's Historical Notes: Contrasted Lives of Jefferson Davis and Abraham Lincoln*, vol. 1 (Athens, GA: self-published, 1927), 1.

13. Carter Godwin Woodson, *The Mis-Education of the Negro* (1933; repr., Chicago: Associated Publishers, 1969), 115.

14. Martin Luther King, Jr., *Where Do We Go from Here: Chaos or Community?* (New York: Harper and Row, 1967).

15. W. E. B. Du Bois, *The Souls of Black Folk* (Chicago: A. C. McClurg & Co., 1903), 109.

16. Catharine A. MacKinnon, *Only Words* (Cambridge, MA: Harvard University Press, 1996), 82.

17. Charles R. Lawrence III, "If He Hollers Let Him Go: Regulating Racist Speech on Campus," *Duke Law Journal* 1990, no. 3 (June 1990): 436.

INDEX

◇

INDEX

INDEX

Jablonski, Nina, 19–20
Jackson, Bruce, 116
Jackson, Jesse, 41
James, Henry, 184
James, William, 166
jazz, 147–50
"Jazz at Home" (Rogers), 150
Jea, John, 27, 83
Jefferson, Thomas, xxvi, 14–16, 20,
    32, 36, 38–39, 43, 135
  Africans dehumanized by, 34
  Banneker and, 29–31
  Walker quoting, 33
  Wheatley, P., dismissed by, 16–17
Jennings, Thomas L., 45–46
Jezebel (stereotype), 106–8
Jim Crow, 101–2
Jocelyn, Simeon S., 61
Johnson, Barbara, xvii, 114
Johnson, James Weldon, 144,
    187, 196
  double consciousness literalized
    by, 168, 194
  Garvey feared by, 139–40
  Harlem Renaissance called for
    by, 134
Johnson, Val Marie, 131
Jones, Gayl, 179
The Journal of American Folklore, 154

Kant, Immanuel, xxvi, 12–13, 19,
    38, 135
Kellermann, François Etienne de,
    xxxiv
Kincaid, Jamaica, 179
King, Martin Luther, Jr., xxvii, 207,
    223
Knight, G. Wilson, 225

The Lady of the Lake (Scott), 80
Langston, John Mercer, 57
Larrimore, George, 86
Larrimore, George, Jr., 87
Latino, Juan "El Negro," 24

law of hypodescent, xv, 189
Lawrence, Charles, 227–28
The Leopard's Spots (Dixon), xxvi
Letters of the Late Ignatius Sancho
    (Sancho), 25
Lewis, David Levering, 109, 128, 130
The Liberator, 53–54, 66, 82
Liberia, emigration to, 46, 50, 57, 77
Life in a Box Is a Pretty Life (Martin),
    xxvii
linguistic separation (myth), 160–61
literacy, 27, 65, 83–84, 98, 213
Lobkowitz (count), xxxiv
Lochner, Norbert, 236n26
Locke, Alain, xxv, 123, 138, 140, 141
Logan, Rayford W., 101
Lost Cause myth, 215–16, 220, 222
Lundy, Benjamin, 59
Lyons, Maritcha, 131

MacKinnon, Catharine, 226
Madison, James, 49
Mammonism, 197–98
Mammy (stereotype), 106–8
The Man Who Lived Underground
    (Wright), xxvi
"March Against Fear" (1966), 41
March on Washington for Jobs and
    Freedom, 208
Marrant, John, 27
The Marrow of Tradition
    (Chesnutt), 125
Marshall, Thurgood, 186
Martin, Dawn Lundy, xxvii
Mason-Dixon Line, 85, 87
Matthews, Victoria Earle, 130,
    133–35, 140–41
McCune Smith, James, 43, 44,
    67–68, 90–91
McDaniel, Hattie, 107
McKay, Claude, 142
A Measuring Rod (Rutherford),
    217–19
Mencken, H. L., xxxvi

INDEX

INDEX